George Boran CSSp

Training Course
for Leaders

First published in 2002 by
the columba press
55A Spruce Avenue, Stillorgan Industrial Park, Blackrock, Co Dublin

Cover by George Boran
Origination by The Columba Press
Printed in Ireland by ColourBooks Ltd, Dublin

ISBN 1 85607 359 9

THE ROAD NOT TAKEN

Two roads diverged in a yellow wood,
And sorry I could not travel both ...

I shall be telling this with a sigh
Somewhere ages and ages hence:
Two roads diverged in a wood, and I,
I took the one less travelled by,
And that has made all the difference.

Robert Frost

Copyright © 2002, George Boran CSSp

TRAINING COURSE FOR LEADERS

Contents

PART 1: INTRODUCTORY COMPONENTS

Introduction	9
Structure of Training Course for Leaders (TCL)	13
Optional timetables:	
a. Timetable for weekend course	14
b. Alternative timetables	17
Form for Preparatory meetings	18
Distribution of functions for Celebration of Commitment	19

PART 2: PREPARATION OF COURSE

How to Organise the Course:	
Functions and method for training the co-ordination team	22

PART 3. DETAILED EXPLANATION

Friday	32
Saturday	40
Sunday	49

PART 4: APPENDICES: LIST OF MATERIAL FOR COURSE

Appendix No 1A:	Weekend Timetable	55
Appendix No 1B:	Alternative Timetable	
	Broken into Smaller Units (for night-time course, classes etc.)	58
Appendix No 1C:	Alternative Timetable: One Day Course	60
Appendix No 1D:	Alternative Timetable: Two Day Course	62
Appendix No 1E:	Alternative Timetable: Three Day Course	64
Appendix No. 2:	Form for preparatory meetings	66
Appendix No. 3:	Prayer to the Holy Spirit	67
Appendix No. 4:	General list of all material used in TCL	68
Appendix No. 5:	Form for indicating possible future facilitators	69
Appendix No. 6:	Explanation folder (for local community, school or other entity)	70
Appendix No. 7:	Model of Booking Form	73
Appendix No. 8:	Objectives of TCL	75

Appendix No. 9:	Johary's Window	77
Appendix No. 10:	Distribution of functions	79
Appendix No. 11:	Traffic Rules (for better communication)	81
Appendix No. 12:	Voting papers for the Sociogramme	83
Appendix No. 13:	Morning Prayer (Saturday)	84
Appendix No. 14A:	Fish Bowl Exercise: Evaluation questions for the Observation Group	85
Appendix No. 14B:	**1st Theme**: GROUP DYNAMICS	86
Appendix No. 14C:	Instructions for the co-ordinators of the Mini-dramas (during the talk on Group Dynamics)	94
Appendix No. 15A:	Instructions for the Observers of the Non-verbal Co-operation exercise	96
Appendix No. 15B:	Text: Competitive Situation – Co-operative Situation	97
Appendix No. 16:	**2nd Theme**: THE DIGNITY OF THE HUMAN PERSON	98
Appendix No. 17A:	**3rd Theme**: JESUS CHRIST	105
Appendix No. 17B:	Preparation of mini-dramas	109
Appendix No. 18A:	Psychological Profile	110
Appendix No. 18B:	Personal notes	112
Appendix No. 18C:	Text: My beloved bamboo	113
Appendix No. 19A:	**4th Theme**: THE CHURCH AS COMMUNITY	115
Appendix No. 19B:	Text: The kingdom always lies beyond us	121
Appendix No. 19C:	Questions for discussion on continuity	122
Appendix No. 20A:	Time Management: self-evaluation	123
Appendix No. 20B:	**5th Theme**: TECHNIQUES OF TIME MANAGEMENT	128
Appendix No. 21A:	Picture for the Social Shortsightness exercise	139
Appendix No. 21B:	Text: The eclipse of the sun	140
Appendix No. 22:	Evaluation of the TCL	141
Appendix No. 23A:	Text: Celebration of Commitment	142
Appendix No. 23B:	Text of the 'Disciples on the Way to Emmaus'	150
Appendix No. 23C:	Functions for the Celebration of Commitment	151
Appendix No. 24:	Form for financial report	152
Appendix No. 25:	Model of badge as Symbol of Commitment	153
Appendix No. 26:	Model of nametag	153
Appendix No. 27:	A Pastoral Experience: Using the TCL as a tool for pastoral renewal	154

PART 1

Introductory Components

Introduction

An Irish girl once said to me: 'All the church has is the Mass, and that is boring.' The statement of this young girl reflects the need for profound change in the church's mission, especially in First World countries. There is a crisis of the traditional pastoral strategies used by the church to transmit the faith from one generation to another. Parish structures, Catholic schools, religious education class, the family, and Sunday Mass no longer have the same capacity to transmit the faith as before. With the change of the culture that sustained a traditional faith, the older formation methods are rapidly losing their ability to attract people, especially the young. It is not the faith that has changed; it is rather the surrounding culture. The change from a rural to an industrialised society and the extraordinary power of the modern electronic means of communication have provoked a cultural change: a change from a pre-modern and Christian culture to a modern and now a post-modern culture where the support structures for faith are no longer present. Before it was easy to be a Christian. The current was taking us in that direction. Now to be a practising Christian a young person has to row against the current. A cultural faith or a family faith will no longer survive in these inauspicious surroundings. Only a personal faith based on personal convictions and supported by some form of community or group experience is able to withstand the strong contrary winds.

Many church leaders, both religious and lay, are confused and dispirited. The 'we-are-dying' syndrome acts like a contagious disease that provokes a heavy cloud of gloom. One priest put it this way: 'In the past we were up in the other half of the field, scoring goal after goal. It was great! Now we are back in our own square and as soon as we get the ball out it is back in again. We have a feeling of being overwhelmed by it all. The old methods are not working any more and we don't have any others.' Many church leaders have been trained to dealing with a captive audience and don't have the leadership skills for going out from the security of the sacristy and 'selling' the Christian message in an attractive way and in a way that is relevant today. While recently discussing this issue with an English Christian I talked of my conviction of the need to train people in the necessary leadership skills, to help them to dream again, to leave the false security of the sacristy, take risks and have the patience to take 'baby steps' at the beginning. She agreed but said I had left out the most important element. 'You also need to believe, to be enthusiastic, to be passionate about the message you have to transmit.' The word gospel means good news. Good news cannot be communicated in a dispirited way. The image of a salesperson trying to sell something that he has absolutely no faith in is very relevant here. The message we have to transmit was never more relevant. However, we just need to figure out how to transmit it in a language that a modern generation can understand.

Sociologists today make a distinction between economic capital and social capital.* Social capital is the relationships and the value system we build up through voluntary organisations and churches and the willingness to help others without being rewarded. Social capital has been built up over centuries and churches have contributed greatly to this. Social capital gives a quality, warmth and energy to our communities and neighbourhoods. Today there is a crisis of values. When we take away religion then we have really nothing in which to root a value system. People ask themselves, 'Why be good? Why think of others? Why not be selfish if I can get away with it?" In Europe and in the United States we have been concentrating on building up economic capital and eating into our social capital. The consequences are serious. Studies done in the US over the last thirty years have shown that this policy is leading to social disintegration with the consequent exclusion of sectors of society, increase in violence, dysfunctional families, loneliness, drop off in membership in volunteer organisations etc are creating a very cold, selfish, greedy and dangerous world for our children.

The Training Course for Leaders (TCL) has been designed to help meet the challenges outlined above.

With the help of a team of dedicated religious and lay leaders I worked with this course for many years, in Brazil and other Latin American countries.

---

* *Bowling Alone* by Robert Putnam (Simon & Schuster)

In all, perhaps over two thousand courses were given. Many suggestions which came from the evaluation meetings that followed each course were incorporated into the original scheme. The initial program, as a result, went through a continuous process of transformation and improvement. So the course, in its present form, has been tested in a very wide variety of pastoral situations. It is not something put together in an office without any reference to real situations. It is a formula that works.

Recently while doing advanced studies in the United States I was invited to be adviser to the Hispanic Youth Ministry in the diocese where I was staying. There were more then 300, 000 people of Latin American origin in the diocese. The diocesan co-ordination team was discouraged. Different events promoted by the members rarely brought together more than 15 to 20 young people. We decided to use this course (TCL) as a strategy to involve parishes, reorganise youth groups, to form new ones, to discover potential leaders and train them.

The strategy worked and we were soon able to organise new diocesan and parish structures where young people were given ownership and became the principal actors in their own education and growth in faith. After the first year of using the course to reach potential leaders, there was a revolution in the level of motivation and dedication of young people, in the training of leaders and in the capacity of the diocesan co-ordination team to mobilise people for important events. This pastoral experience is recounted in appendix 27. As a tool for renewing parish and diocesan structures this experience has served as a reference for other dioceses and parishes. While this experience deals mainly with young people the course has been equally successful with adults.

As part of the adaptation process of this course to a European context, we gave three courses in Dublin (over a period of two years). The first course was given to a mainly adult audience from a parish background, the second course was given to young people from different parts of the country and the third course was given as a module for students in a secondary school who were doing the Transition Year.

Description of the Course

The course is built around five main themes:
 • Group dynamics;
 • The Dignity of the Human Person;
 • Jesus Christ and being a Christian;
 • The Church as community and as a sign and service to the world;
 • Techniques of Time Management.

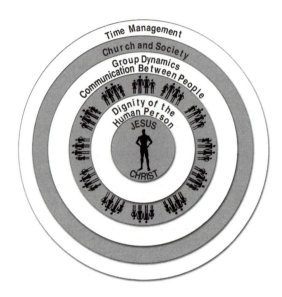

A wide variety of exercises are used to awaken people to a sense of responsibility and initiative. The combination of talks and exercises aim at helping participants to think for themselves. The ethos of the course presupposes that a leader who cannot think for himself or herself is not a leader. In this way the course proposes an alternative road to the many forms of manipulation, massification and domestication that are prevalent in society today. We are proposing a road less travelled and we believe that, for those who take it, it will make all the difference.

In recent years there has been a shift from courses with many talks and passive audiences to courses where the emphasis is on growth through participation. However these courses, in order to create greater participation and sharing by the participants, have frequently restricted themselves to a single exercise: group discussion – plenary session – group discussion – plenary session. This solution quickly becomes monotonous and tiresome. The present course avoids this danger by using a wide variety of exercises that make it a lively and joyful learning experience.

While the Training Course for Leaders (TCL) can be used with beginners to discover and train potential future leaders it can also be used with people who are already involved. The values that are presented are important for all levels of commitment.

Objectives of the Course

- Train people for team work
- Facilitate self knowledge
- Build self-confidence
- Acquire the skills of interpersonal communication
- Learn the skills of time management
- Develop a critical sense
- Develop a spirituality that gives unity to life
- Make a personal option for Jesus Christ
- Create deeper bonds and promote an experience of church as community
- Develop a value system that gives direction to our lives
- Help people to move towards commitment
- Form Leaders

The course has a number of advantages over other programmes:

A. It uses a unique methodology
- The programme uses a strategy of training people who can give the course themselves in their own communities or schools. In this way a greater number of people can be reached in a shorter time-span. This strategy builds on a basic educational principle that the best way of acquiring new knowledge is by being required to teach it to others.
- The course uses a methodology of creating learning situations where participants learn by doing. An important educational principle is at work here: the lessons that we remember best and that become part of our lives are the lessons we teach ourselves.
- A special method for training facilitators is used.
- It also has the advantage of being easily reproduced at a very low cost.
- The course does not compete with but rather fits into and complements other programmes.

B. It can be used in a variety of flexible ways
- It can be given as a week end experience (either in a retreat house or returning home at night time).
- It can be broken up into smaller units and used as a resource kit for religion class, for meetings, for short formation courses, for Transition Year in school.
- It can be given to beginners or to people who have already taken on different commitments, on local or wider levels.

C. The TCL can be given to a variety of groups:
- To leaders who are involved with different church, social or cultural activities, either on diocesan or local levels.
- To people from the same community;
- To youth and adults together;
- To adults only
- To students and teachers from the same school;
- To transition year students
- To youth who are preparing for or have finished confirmation.

For a variety of reasons specialists are frequently not available to help in formation programmes. At the same time, people involved in church work seek more practical tools to help them in their formation programmes. They lack a kind of 'do-it-yourself' kit. This is all the more important today as trends in a post-modern culture emphasise the need for concrete activities that give immediate results. Initial success is important to motivate people to take further steps on the road to commitment and conversion.

The TCL has further advantages. It can be easily reproduced at a low cost (in terms of finances and personnel) in order to reach a large number of people over a short period of time. Without this type of strategy we run the risk of seeing our pastoral work being reduced to a small group of discouraged individuals who believe they are wasting their time rowing against the current trends in an individualist and materialistic post-modern cultural environment.

This style of course has the advantage of involving lay people in a way that they are no longer treated as passive listeners in the church but rather as co-responsible for communicating the good news of the gospel to others. This strategy is especially influential with young people. A young person, speaking to other young people can have more influence than a priest, a sister or parents. The power of peer pressure can be channelled in a positive way.

One of the major challenges facing the church in many modern environments is the exit from the church of youth after confirmation. While confirmation is defined as the sacrament of commitment it is increasingly the official and solemn liturgical ceremony in which many adolescents begin the process of distancing themselves from the church.

The perseverance rate of the youth who have done this course, in preparation for confirmation or immediately afterwards has been high. The emotional links created during the course can lead to the formation of youth groups or other forms of participation that guarantee continuity after the reception of the sacrament. The course can be given either on a weekend or broken up into different 'classes' as part of the wider programme of preparation for the sacrament.

The course can be given to youth or adults separately, but also for a group that has a mixture of adults and youth. The mixture of adults and youth is especially effective. The TCL is one of the few tools for overcoming the generation gap and bringing youth and adults together from the same parish community or school. The different exercises and the experience of doing the course together open up channels of communication and build a climate of confidence that is important in any sort of church or social ministry.

The TCL can be given in a retreat centre where participants are not obliged to return home at nighttime. Living together, over a weekend, leads to greater bonding and more time is available for discussion and study. However, where costs are a major problem, the course can be given in the local parish or school. At night time participants can sleep at home.

Where it is difficult to get people together for a weekend, the course can be spread out over five night sessions during the week.

When a community or pastoral ministry show interest in scheduling the TCL, appendix No 6 (Explanation Folder for the local community, school or other entity that have requested the course) can be used to explain what is involved.

In writing this book I have tried to deal with the question of inclusive language in a way that would facilitate the flow of ideas. For that reason I have generally avoided using such clumsy phrases as 'he and she' and 'her and his' and adopted a general strategy of using the feminine pronouns in some paragraphs and the masculine ones in others.

Sequence of steps in training

The method of training the Co-ordination Team is perhaps the most innovating aspect of this book. A description of the steps in this method can be found in the chapter, *How to Organise the Course, Functions and method for Training the Co-ordination Team*. The method of training is that of apprenticeship, of learning by doing, of learning by experience. This is more effective than an exclusively theoretical method.

During the course talks are complemented by exercises where people can learn through a process of trial and error, while relying on the orientation of someone with greater experience. This is the way a person normally learns a profession. One does not form a surgeon with conferences and readings. This is the way we learn the leadership skills necessary to answer the call of Jesus: 'Go and evangelise all people.'

The course aims at providing an experience of a living Christian community rather than the mere passing on of theoretical knowledge. The TCL does not offer a magic solution for the challenges facing the church's mission in a post-modern age. It can however be an important tool for renewal. It can complement other programmes. It can also be an important initial step for starting a process of involving people on increasingly wider levels and changing a climate of defeatism to one of hope and enthusiasm.

George Boran CSSp

Structure of the Course

GROUP DYNAMICS
    Johary's Window
    Distribution of functions
    Traffic rules
    Sociogramme 1
    Liturgy
    Presentation of functions
    Fishbowl exercise
    1st Theme: Group dynamics

DIGNITY OF THE HUMAN PERSON
    Non-verbal co-operation exercise
    2nd Theme: Dignity of the human person
    Sociogramme II

JESUS CHRIST
    3rd Theme: Study of text: 'Jesus Christ'
    Plenary session
    'Spirit of a Mule' exercise
    Mini-dramas on gospel texts
    Sociogramme III
    Plenary session
    Psychological profile

CHURCH – COMMUNITY OF PEOPLE
    Prayer
    Presentation of functions
    4th Theme: The church, a community of people
    Debate on continuity
    Test: Time management – self evaluation
    5th Theme: Techniques of time management
    Social short-sightedness exercise
    Revision
    Evaluation of course
    Celebration of commitment

TECHNIQUES OF TIME MANAGEMENT
    Test: Time Management – Self Evaluation
    5th Theme: Techniques of Time Management

Timetable for a Weekend Course

Place: _____

Date: _____

Co-ordination Team:

Team Leader: …………………………..

Member 1:………………………………

Member 2:………………………………

Member 3:………………………………

FRIDAY *Facilitator Responsible*

19:30 (30)	Arrival, Reception, welcome, Nametags etc.	___

20:00 (30)	Prayer and Introduction.
	Presentation:
	    The team and participants
	    The objectives (Appendix 8)
	    How the course works
		___

20.30 (30)	Johary's Window (Appendix 9)	___
21.00 (30)	Distribution of Functions (Appendix 10)	___
21.30 (45)	Traffic Rules (Appendix 11)	___
22.15 (15)	Sociogramme I (Appendix 12)	___
22.30 (05)	Closure *Notices:* Timetable for the following day, preparation of functions for the next session, importance of being present for the entire course, time for lights out, fines etc.	___

INTRODUCTORY PART

SATURDAY   *Facilitator*
                                                            Responsible

08.45 (30)	Morning Prayer (Appendix 13)	——
09.15 (30)	Free time to finish preparation of functions	
09.45 (45)	Presentation of functions	——
10.30 (15)	Result of Sociogramme I	——
10.45 (15)	Break	
11.00 (30)	Exercise: Fish-bowl debate (Appendix 14A)	——
11.30 (45)	1st Theme: Talk: 'Group Dynamics' (Appendixes 14B, 14C)	——
11.45 (45)	Exercise: Non-verbal Co-operation (Appendixes 15A & 15B)	——
12.30 (10)	Sociogramme II (voting)	——
12.40 ( )	Lunch: 'Spirit of a Mule' (optional)	——
14.00 (45)	2nd Theme: Talk: 'Dignity of the Human Person' (Appendix 16A)	——
14.45 (30)	Result of Sociogramme II	——
15.15 (45)	3rd Theme: Study of text & debate: 'Jesus Christ and being a Christian' (Appendix 17A)	——
16.00 (30)	Break	
16.30 (30)	Plenary session (The principal ideas of the groups should be written down on a blackboard and then a debate can follow)	——
17.00 (15)	Sociogramme III (voting)	——
17.15 (30)	Preparation of mini-dramas (Appendix 17B)	
17.45 (30)	Plenary session	——
18.15 (60)	Supper	
19.15 (90?)	Psychological Profile (Appendixes 18A, 18B, 18C) Closure	—

Side tab: JESUS CHRIST   HUMAN PERSON   GROUP DYNAMICS

SUNDAY   *Facilitator*
                                                                          Responsible

| | 0 8.45 (15) | Morning Prayer | ___ |

CHURCH

- 09.00 (45)   Presentation of functions   ___

- 09.45 (45)   4th Theme: Talk: 'Church as a Community
                     of Believers' (Appendixes 19A, 19B)   ___

- 10.30 (30)   Break

- 11.00 (45)   Plenary Session: Debate on questions related to church
                     and continuity (Appendix 19C)   ___

TIME MANAGEMENT

- 11.45 (30)   Test: Time Management: Self Evaluation (Appendix 20A)   ___

- 12.15 (60)   Lunch

- 13.15 (60)   5th Theme: Techniques of Time Management (Appendix 20B)
                     (improving the quality of your life
                     and the efficacy of your action)   ___

- 14.15 (15)   Exercise: Social Shortsightedness
                     (Appendixes 21A, 21B, 21C)   ___

CONCLUSION

- 15.00 (30)   Revision   ___

- 15.15 (30)   Evaluation (Appendix 22)   ___

- 15.45 (15)   Singing Practice   ___

- 16.00 (90)   Celebration of commitment (Mass or Celebration of the Word)
               (Appendixes 23A, 23B, 23C)   ___

- 17.30   Closure

Alternative Timetables

*1. Course Broken into Smaller Units
(for night-time course, classes etc.)*
Timetable
See Appendix No 1B

*2. Course Given during School Curriculum
e.g. Module for Transition Year*

a. One Day Course
Timetable
See Appendix No 1C

a. Two Day Course
Timetable
See Appendix No 1D

a. Three Day Course
Timetable
See Appendix No 1E

Form for Preparatory Meetings

Entity requesting the Course:_____

Date of Course:_____

Co-ordination Team:

Team Leader:

_____

Members:

_____
_____
_____
_____

PROGRAMMING OF PREPARATORY EVENTS	PERIOD	DATE	TIME
1. Definition of place, price, etc.	9 weeks beforehand		
2. Printing and distribution of Invitation forms	9 weeks beforehand		
3. 1st Training session of team/ distribution of functions	2 months beforehand		
4. Meeting with the local community & Logistics' Commission	7 weeks beforehand		
5. 2nd Training session of team	1 month beforehand		
6. Return of Invitation Forms	3 weeks beforehand		
7. 3rd Training session of team	2 weeks beforehand		
8. 4th Meeting (when necessary): unfinished business	?		
9. Date for giving the Course			
10. Meeting for Evaluation / indication of future facilitators			

Distribution of Functions for Celebration of Commitment

Functions:

    General Co-ordinator: _____

    President of Celebration (celebrant): _____

    Preparation of setting: _____

    Initial welcome: _____

    Penitential Rite: _____

    Biblical Reading: _____

    Sound: _____

    Overhead projector: _____

    Singing: _____

    Ceremony of sending on mission: _____

    Symbols for the offertory procession: _____

Preparation of material:

    Tape recorder, CD, cassettes
    Overhead projector
    Material for flame: 2 clay vessels, fibre glass, one litre of alcohol,
    One small bowl with olive oil or some other type of oil
    Small basket with the symbols of commitment
    Transparencies with the gospel reading and with different coloured pictures
        or images and the final blessing
    Preparation of setting for Mass: necessary material for the Mass, rugs,
        tapestry, flowers, posters etc.

PART 2

Preparation of the Course

How to organise the Course: Functions and Method for Training the Co-ordination Team

Team Leader: The co-ordination team is made up of 4 or 5 facilitators, one of whom has the function of Team Leader. Not all the facilitators will have conditions for taking on this function. The Team Leader is the key to the success of the course. He should have vision of the whole; be able to work with many things at the same time; be able to motivate and encourage the other members to give the best of themselves; be able to give attention to the task of the moment and at the same time think ahead; know how to manage conflicts and tensions between members, so the environment of friendship and joy in the course is not harmed. The Team Leader supervises the organising and the steps that lead up to the course and is concerned that the members of the team are well trained. Obviously, as the members of the team grow in maturity and experience many of these functions will be taken on by others. If for some reason the Team Leader is not up to the task, the other members of the team should move in to make up for his lack of ability or motivation.

The principal function of the Team Leader is to train well the other facilitators. He needs to be able to detect when a task, an exercise or talk has been badly prepared. He should insist that each facilitator present his task as if he is applying it in the course. The training session should simulate the real situation. It begins with the statement: 'Imagine that you are now in the course and we are the participants – apply now your exercise or task.' In this way faults in the understanding and preparation of the facilitator will surface. Obviously it is better that these faults come to the surface in the training session rather than during the course itself.

The Treasurer: In each course one of the facilitators should take on the responsibility for looking after finances and making out a financial report at the end. Appendix 38 was prepared to facilitate this task. The formation of leadership involves training people to administer in an honest and professional way the money of others. We cannot criticise the lack of ethics and corruption in public life if in our pastoral ministry there is not a transparent administration of the resources of colleagues.

During each course, the co-ordination team should

be attentive to detect people who can be trained as new facilitators. In this way, in each new course, one or two new candidates can be integrated into the group of facilitators that are available for giving future courses. When a sufficient number of facilitators has been trained, it is possible to schedule courses on dates that suit best the groups or communities that are interested and so avoid overburdening a few people.

The facilitators who form part of the co-ordination team need to take into account two things.
a. Skills, attitudes and options that need to be present in their lives if the course is to work well.
b. Important organisational details that should not be forgotten.

A. SKILLS, ATTITUDES AND OPTIONS

The exercises don't work automatically. The people who apply the exercises should, have a psychological sensitivity for dealing with other people, the capacity to observe, to work in a team and have a renewed theological and pastoral vision. It is fundamental to:

Create a climate of confidence
It is important that the team responsible for the course be open and friendly on first contact, creating in this way a climate of acceptance and confidence.

Know how to apply the exercises
The objective of some exercises should not be explained before they are applied. In these cases the explanation is given at the end. Since the aim of the exercises in question is to provoke the participants to think and discover for themselves, the revelation of the objective will weaken the effect of these exercises.

On the other hand, the nature of the other exercises demands that the objective be explained in advance. In these cases, the explanation is necessary for the application of the exercises.
With the explanation of each exercise there is a notice indicating the need to explain or not the objective before its application. After each exercise, the person responsible should ask the participants to link the lessons learned with their real life situations (parish community, school, work, recreational, and social situation) so that a union between faith and life is established.

Frequently the facilitators of this course need to undergo a conversion from a traditional methodology that we have been formed in. The formation many of us have received in the family, in school, in politics, and in the church has been paternalist. We have been trained in a methodology of doing things 'from the top down'. We are used to receiving everything ready made. We have been trained to give orders, to talk at people rather than listen. Almost all of our social organisation is built on paternalism and this makes it difficult for people to take on responsibility for their own lives and for building a better world.

This course presents a different pedagogical proposal – that of forming leaders; people who can think for themselves, who are subjects of their own destiny and who have a critical awareness of what is taking place in the surrounding society. In order for this new pedagogical proposal to work it is not enough to change our discourse. Our practice and our way of working with others must also change. In this course, for example, it is not enough for a facilitator to give a good talk on Group Dynamics and how to work in a team, if in real life situations he is not a team person.

The secret is in the preparation
The mission of the facilitators is to prepare the soil so that when the seed of the Word of God falls it can germinate and produce much fruit. Success depends on the grace of God, but also on the preparation of the facilitators. Each facilitator needs to prepare well before the course. But remote preparation is not sufficient. During the course she needs to be alert and not neglect immediate preparation during the period that precedes the presentation of her exercise. She needs to concentrate, to pick up where the group is at and not be dispersed or scattered at the moment of entering into communication with the group.

Therefore, the secret of a good facilitator is in the preparation. The exercises and talks need to be well prepared before the course by each members of the co-ordination team. When the facilitator is clear about the objective and the steps in the application of the exercise, she transmits confidence and tranquillity to the participants. Even when one has prepared well beforehand, it is important to give a last look, to refresh one's memory, before applying an exercise. It is obvious that an exercise has greater effect when the facilitator doesn't need to read each step mechanically when applying it.

Spirituality of the Facilitator
We are instruments in the hands of God. Preparation and talents are important. However, only God can touch deeply the heart of each participant. We are privileged to have received his call: 'Go and evangelise all peoples.' Before applying an exercise or giving a talk it is necessary to enter in contact with God who is present in the depth of our being so that this divine energy can contaminate the people with whom we are working. Our principal aim is to help the participants meet with Jesus Christ on a personal level, through the exercises, talks, personal witness and a community experience. As facilitators we are not – and should not be – the centre. The model for each facilitator is John the Baptist who insisted that, with the coming of Jesus, 'I must diminish so that he can increase.' (Jn 3:30).

Know how to manage time
The TCL has a characteristic that distinguishes it from other encounters – everything is timed, even the details. An initial observation is important here. Not every course has to be this way. It is not the only model; there are other models, of course, where there is less concern with time. In our formation programmes, a balance between different types of courses is healthy. So while this model gives excellent results, we are not proposing that it be the only model in our pastoral ministry.

The capacity to administer and control time in the TCL is a central factor in its success. Friday night is perhaps the most difficult part of the course. Time is very limited due to the impossibility of starting earlier. Many participants arrive after a day's work or a day at school. At the same time there are exercises that need to be applied and content that needs to be assimilated in order to have a foundation on which to build during the following days. In compensation the Sunday timetable is easier.

The lack of control of the timetable can have serious consequences for the success of the course, for example, the co-ordination team may be obliged to start on Saturday morning without the necessary foundation – or later during the course important parts may have to be eliminated due to lack of time – or the Saturday session may end far too late. The incapacity of the co-ordination team to administer time can have a high price. Nevertheless, a certain flexibility may be necessary. Circumstances may dictate the necessity to cut some exercises in the course.

There are different talks during the course: Johary's Window, Group Dynamics, The Dignity of the Human Person, the Church as a Community of People, Techniques of Time Management. Speakers can easily be carried away by the topic they are addressing and fail to take into account the time available. We recommend that a member of the team be responsible for discretely showing cards indicating the time that is left (e.g. 15 minutes, 10 minutes, 5 minutes, 00 minutes) so that speakers can more easily control the time allotted to them.

Despite the concern with time, the co-ordination team needs to be flexible: there are moments in which it may be necessary to prolong a debate and there are others in which it may be necessary to cut things.

There is a further advantage to this type of course. The effort to manage time helps the members of the co-ordination team acquire important skills and discipline for their work as leaders in the different pastoral ministries. One of the factors that jam the smooth running of much of church work is the many meeting that have neither a time for starting nor ending, where the agenda is not prepared in advance and where there is no method to give direction to the discussion. The lack of planning and the superficiality of many our meetings lead many people to abandon active involvement in the church. Many courses and encounters also follow a style that is often improvised and superficial. There is a feeling of wasting time. The cultural change brought about by the post-modern culture has created a generation that has a low of tolerance for monotony and superficiality. There are many other attractive proposals in today's society to fill in time.

Also, people have little time available. Their time is taken up with many issues related to work, family, school, sports and social life. The time that is left over for involvement in church and social work is small. We have to use well the little time that is available. Time management means, also, that we have more time for relaxation and meeting people. In this way we can avoid burnout, a factor often present in the lives of many people today.

The capacity to anticipate events
The success of the course also depends on the capacity of facilitators to anticipate events. To do so, they need to have one eye on the tasks immediately following and the other eye on the long-term tasks that need to be anticipated or perhaps changed (in relation to the timetable, for example). Otherwise, they may find themselves approaching the end of the day several hours behind in the timetable and being obliged to cut important parts of the course.

Individual Accompaniment
Each member of the co-ordination team is responsible for a number of participants and makes a point of being available if they have any doubts that may arise about their functions.

Critical sense
The function of the facilitators consists in not only transmitting knowledge to the participants. Their primary function is to help the participants to think for themselves, to discover, and together to arrive at a critical awareness of the reality that is around them and of their role as Christians within this reality.

The course should provide experience of a living Christian community rather than the mere passing on of theoretical knowledge, incapable of changing people, situation and society. Theory is important in so far as it is linked to real life situations.

The importance of being coherent
The members of the co-ordination team should be coherent. They should be enthusiastic and convinced about the message they are transmitting. They are mindful that one of the obstacles to evangelisation is 'the apathy and especially the lack of joy and hope in many of our evangelisers'. (EN 79) The values and techniques presented in the course should be part of the lives of those applying them. Words impress while example leads to change and conversion. If we propose to form lay people as leaders who can think for themselves, we must be trying to apply this principle in our own lives. This means that, in our own pastoral work with others, we are not threatened when new leaders emerge and take initiatives without our permission. Our aim is avoid creating dependencies, to form leaders not followers. A phrase of Paul VI captures the modern mentality: 'The people of our day are more impressed by witness than by teachers, and if they listen to these it is because they also bear witness.' (EN 41)

B. ORGANISATIONAL DETAILS

The co-ordination team needs to take into account the following issues when preparing a course:

Meeting with local representatives
On reception of a request for a course, members of the co-ordination team can meet with representatives of the community, organisation or school requesting the course to explain the objectives and their role in the preparatory phase. In this meeting the contents of the text of Appendix 7 (Explanation Folder) can be distributed and explained. It may be necessary to organise a logistics commission with some local people – especially when meals need to be cooked. It is important to involve a parish, a local community, a church organisation or school in the organisation of the course. When everything is done by persons from outside, without the participation of the local community, motivation and continuity are more problematic.

It is also important that the contact people from the community or organisation requesting the course be responsible and influential people and can be easily contacted by telephone, fax, e-mail etc during the period that precedes the course. There are always last minute questions to be resolved. With efficient channels of communications many difficulties can be avoided.

Schedule the chronological sequence of steps that precede the course (See Appendix 2)

Prepare the Booking Forms
The forms should include: the date, the place, the price, date for returning the Invitation Form, time for arriving on the first day and time for finishing on the last day, the need to bring a New Testament, etc. The form should also emphasise the importance of being present for the entire course. (See Model of Booking Form, Appendix 7). The booking form should include a tear-off slip which can be returned with the course contribution. It needs to be clearly stated where and when the returned slips will be accepted. The forms should be returned at least a fortnight beforehand so that the organising team can have an idea of the number and type of persons who will participate in the course.

Marketing the Course
The advertising of the course is very important. The attitude of going out to bring in people is especially difficult in a 'sacristy' church accustomed to working with a captive audience. This attitude worked in a previous age, but is no longer viable in a modern and post-modern age where our message is one among many.

This is often the most difficult and important part of the course. People's lives are cluttered up today with many things. We have to be able to convince them that the course will provide something important for their lives otherwise it fails before it starts. This means the minimum of professionalism in the way we present the course. An attractive brochure or booking form should be prepared well in advance. Ways to advertise can include brochure, poster, local radio, newsletter, church notices, perhaps a short explanation at Sunday Mass, in schools, etc. Advertising the course is important to create an attractive environment where a one-to-one invitation can be made. The one-to-one invitation, however, is the key to success. In previous TCL courses we have discovered that over 90% of participants came because a friend or an acquaintance invited them. People will more readily participate when they know that acquaintances or friends will be present. We should be aware of the psychological difficulty of many of going to an event of this nature where there the participants are all strangers.

Prepare and photocopy the hymns (religious and popular songs) to be used during the course.

Combine with someone to take a photograph of the participants to be distributed at the end of the course (optional).

Provide the necessary items for the Celebration of Commitment: altar, wine, hosts, chalice, missal, hymns, place of celebration, symbols of commitment, the book with this course (to be given with the symbol of commitment to each participant at the end of the celebration. (See Appendix 23A). When no priest is available a Celebration of the Word can be organised.

Prepare folders and nametags (with both the name and number in large print so they can be visible from a distance)

Provide old magazines, newspapers, scissors, sticking gum and poster paper for the different exercises.

Have some New Testaments as a reserve in case participants forget to bring theirs.

Separate the different appendixes to be distributed during the course, hymn sheets, sheets for notetaking, folders etc.

Methodology for Training the Team of Facilitators

The method for training follows these steps:

1. *Flexible timetable*
   The timetable of the course can vary, depending on the needs of the group that make the request. Therefore the co-ordination team will make out a fresh timetable for each course. The timetable presented in the book should be photocopied to facilitate adaptations. (See Appendix 1A)

2. *Special folders*
   To facilitate the work of the co-ordination team, the pages of the book can be taken out and placed in plastics in a folder. The appendix for each exercise can be placed in a plastic beside its explication in the section called *Detailed Explanations of the Exercises*. In this way it is easier to locate texts in a hurry during the course. A large number of appendixes are used, so if there is not a good system for organising them, a certain confusion and panic are inevitable. This suggestion of using folders gives a greater flexibility for adapting the course to local needs. This book, together with the symbol of commitment, may be given to each participant at the end the final celebration.

It will be necessary to photocopy the following appendices during the course: Appendices 10, 11, 12, 13, 15B, 17A, 18A, 18B, 18C, 19B, 20A, 21B, 22 (copies for all participants) and Appendices 14A, 14C, 15A, 17B, 23A (a small number of copies according to orientation of different texts). Handouts of the rest of the material are not necessary and could have the effect of discouraging notetaking by the participants. A capacity to take notes is the first step to being able to organise our ideas and develop clear goals. Participants will receive the book at the end and so will have the full content of the course for later study.

Training Sessions

We suggest the following sequence for the training sessions to prepare the TCL:

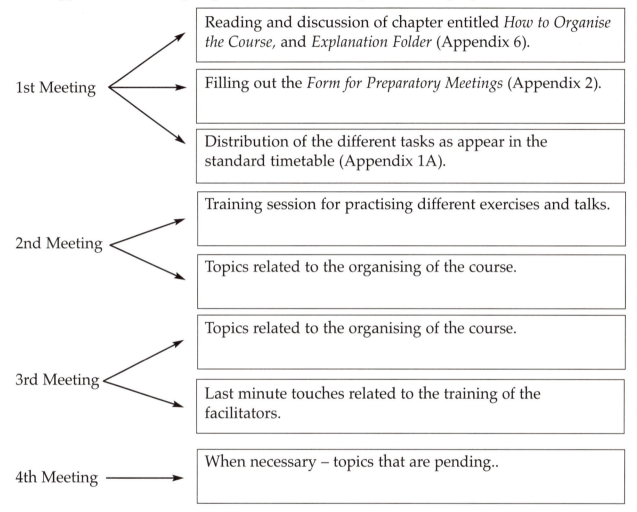

1st Meeting
- Reading and discussion of chapter entitled *How to Organise the Course,* and *Explanation Folder* (Appendix 6).
- Filling out the *Form for Preparatory Meetings* (Appendix 2).
- Distribution of the different tasks as appear in the standard timetable (Appendix 1A).

2nd Meeting
- Training session for practising different exercises and talks.
- Topics related to the organising of the course.

3rd Meeting
- Topics related to the organising of the course.
- Last minute touches related to the training of the facilitators.

4th Meeting
- When necessary – topics that are pending..

The first training session

It is important to help the facilitators to understand that the method used by the TCL is different from other courses and retreats with which they may be accustomed. The course uses an inductive method of helping participants to grow through a process of discovering together rather than giving out readymade recipes. Facilitators who are accustomed to using to a 'top-down' methodology need to go through a pedagogical conversion.

This book is distributed to the members of the co-ordination team and the training session begins with the reading and discussion of the chapter, *How to Prepare the Course: Functions and Method for Training the Co-ordination Team* and Appendix 6 (*Explanation Folder*). The second step is to schedule the next preparatory meetings for the course by filling in Appendix 3 (*Form for Preparatory Meetings*).

As a third step, in this first meeting, a photocopy of the standard timetable (Appendix 1) is read and the exercises, talks and other tasks are distributed among the members of the co-ordination team. The facilitators now have the task of studying the entire book at home, while giving special attention to the tasks that have been allotted to them.

The second meeting will be a training session. The method used is that of learning by doing. The Team Leader asks each member to apply his exercise and, when it is the case, practice his talk, as if they were in the course. The person presenting his task is asked to pretend that the other members of the team are participants in the course. The training session simulates the real situation. It is the same as practising for a play. The actor doesn't just give a general description of what he is going to do. He has to act out his part as if he were on the stage in front of his audience.

This method of training the facilitators is much more powerful than limiting the meeting to a general explanation of the different exercises and talks. Doubts, errors of interpretation and difficulties surface when the exercises are applied and the talks are practised. Obviously, it is better to discover the difficulties before rather than during the course. The role of the Team Leader is essential during the training session. She questions the lack of clarity when a theme is presented, the absence of important steps in the explanation of an exercise, the tendency to change to a more paternalist method, of giving a readymade answer that does not facilitate the process of discovering and of developing the capacity to think for oneself. The Team Leader should resist the temptation to break the embarrassing moments of silence by immediately giving the right answer or by quickly moving on to another topic. Allow the facilitators who have not prepared well to feel the embarrassment of being confused about their task – the feeling of panic because one has not prepared and must now perform in public. It is better to feel ill at ease now rather than during the course when it is no longer possible to correct mistakes. Allow facilitators time to discover where they have gone wrong. This method of preparation gives to the facilitator an apprenticeship, a security and a confidence that are important for the development and success of the course.

During the training sessions, the facilitators should have a notebook for writing important observations that will improve the application of their tasks. Observations that are not written down are forgotten and the same mistakes are repeated in the course. For example, the facilitator who presents the objectives of the course on the first day, needs to discuss with the other members of the team the best way of linking the objectives to the lives and needs of the participants and show their importance for personal growth, for the strengthening of the community, and for building a better world.

In the same way the speaker who explains 'Johary's Window', on the first night, should bring out the importance of each 'window' with examples taken from people's lives, so that the talk does not become an academic exercise – an exercise that is unrelated to the concrete situations of their environment. Therefore, the facilitator who is presenting his task should write down, in his notebook, the ideas of the other members of the team. In this way, important suggestions are not forgotten. In each new training session, we don't have the sensation that we are starting all over again and that suggestions are a waste of time because they are largely ignored anyway.

When facilitators are not well prepared and the day of the course arrives, there is a sensation of panic. They are not clear on what they have to do and realise they are not going to fool people with idle talk. This insecurity will automatically be transmitted to the participants. As each part of the course is presented, important points and observations are left out, thus weakening the overall effect. At the moment of writing, many training sessions come to mind in which the facilitators completely ignored the suggestions and observations made at previous meetings. Since no notes were taken, suggestions were forgotten almost immediately afterwards. There is a feeling of frustration and a sensation of superficiality as exercises are applied mechanically, without concern for their efficacy and content.

The facilitators acquire important skills through this method of training, through the process of preparing and giving the course: the ability to concentrate, to read and understand texts, organise their ideas, communicate with clarity, personal organisation and time management, putting proposals into practice, of systematic follow-up, of self-confidence, of capacity to co-ordinate and become involved. Since we are dealing with a generation that has been strongly influenced by television and the image and have not the custom of serious reading, many facilitators have difficulty in reading a text and grasping the principal ideas. On the other hand, a leader who does not develop the capacity to read is not a leader. This strategy of training has been an important step forward to answer this lacuna.

This second level of training (being required to give the course to others), therefore, has an important effect on the facilitators themselves. The training not only prepares them for transmitting leadership skills to the participants in the course, but also for applying them to different situations in their own lives. The skills learned are automatically transferred to other situations. The acquisition of these skills modifies their way of working with others. As a result facilitators become important leaders in different church and social organisations.

We are talking here of a dynamic method of learning, of learning by doing. It is a much more efficient method that the common method of 'giving talks'. I have given many talks throughout my life on leadership skills and have often been discouraged on discovering later that nothing changed. I discovered that talks need to be complemented by practice so that people can learn through a process of trial and error and, at the same time, be helped by someone with greater experience, in an apprenticeship-like situation

Evaluation meeting after the course
Both the dates of the preparatory meetings and the evaluation meeting after the TCL should be scheduled at the beginning (Appendix 2, *Form for Preparatory Meetings*). Evaluation is important. Not to evaluate is to cease growing. The evaluation meeting is the tool that guarantees that the course is tuned in to the real needs of the participants and avoids superficiality and the mechanical application of techniques that have been emptied of any content. Without constant evaluation the facilitators are condemned to repeat the errors of the past.

During the course the facilitators should take notes of important observations and suggestions to be brought up at the evaluation meeting. We talked earlier about the importance of each facilitator having a notebook. That which is not written down is frequently forgotten. We suggest the following plan of evaluation:

Reading the written evaluations done by the participants or summary of the same.

Evaluation of each facilitator by the other members of the team after having first recalled his/her different tasks during the course. It is important to avoid generic evaluations that fail to indicate the concrete errors to be corrected. In the end, the facilitator being evaluated makes his or her own autoevaluation.

General evaluation of the course.

Final prayer

How to proceed when there is a need to organise many courses at the same time
The leader in a pastoral ministry, in a school or other organisation who decides to use the TCL as a priority tool to strengthen the different pastoral ministries, needs a plan for increasing the number of facilitators and courses without losing quality. With the increase in the number of courses, it will no longer be possible for one leader to accompany all the meetings and all the facilitators. The following plan has been tested and has given good results:

1st Phase: The church or school leader (priest, sister or lay person) accompanies all the courses and training sessions.

2nd Phase. The goal is to multiply multipliers, or train trainers in order reach more people and have a significant impact on the many people who are largely untouched by the gospel values.
a. Selection of Team Leaders who can take on responsibility for different teams of facilitators.
b. General training sessions for Team Leaders and facilitators together. Reading, explication and discussion of chapter entitled *Functions and Method for Training the Co-ordination Team*.
Meeting of each team of facilitators with its respective Team Leader to distribute the different tasks, exercises and talks to be prepared.
Each team plans the steps for preparing its course: schedule all the Training sessions (Appendix 2, *Form for Preparatory Meetings*), prepare and distribute the Booking Forms, schedule a meeting with the local community (Appendix 6, *Explanation Folder*) etc.

3rd Phase. Periodic meetings of Team Leaders and potential Team Leaders to exchange ideas and experiences and to improve their skills.

PART 3

Detailed Explanation of Training Course for Leaders

Detailed Explanations of the Different Exercises

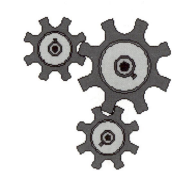

FRIDAY

19.30 (60): Arrival and snack

Facilitator: ....

- Nametags and folders are given out as the participants arrive. The names should be written out in large, readable letters. A different number for each participant is also written on the bottom corner of the nametag. Both the names and numbers should be visible at a distance.
- The co-ordination team should welcome warmly people as they arrive and possibly introduce them to others. Remember many people may be apprehensive, shy and even fearful about this first contact.
- Special care should be taken to create the right ambience in the room where the course will take place. Simple touches such as background music, flowers, a banner or poster, a table with cloth, and seating arrangements can create positive first impressions.

20.15-20. 45 (30): Beginning and Introduction

Facilitator: ....

This first section is divided into four parts:
    a. brief prayer session
    b. presentation of co-ordination team and the participants
    c. presentation of the objectives
    d. how the course works

a. Brief prayer session

b. Presentation of co-ordination team and the participants
    1. Presentation of co-ordination team.
    2. Presentation of participants:
a. The facilitator explains the importance of trying to memorise the names of participants in the session which will follow. Names are important. If someone forgets our name we feel hurt. If, on the other hand, a person remembers our name after only a fleeting acquaintance we feel uplifted and valued. Emotional links are immediately created. Communication is easier.
b. The facilitator asks the participants to present themselves, giving their name, pastoral experience, expectations for the course, favourite sports team, etc.
c. To memorise the names the following technique can be used. Individuals present themselves spontaneously again, saying, 'my name is …' and then point in the direction of someone whose name they have forgotten and ask 'what is your name?' The

session can continue until participants are reasonably satisfied they have memorised most of the names. This can be an important icebreaker for melting the tension and fear felt on the first night in the midst of strangers.

c. Presentation of the objectives of the course

One of the facilitators explains the following objectives of the course:
- Train people for team work
- Facilitate self-knowledge
- Build self-confidence
- Acquire the skills of interpersonal communication
- Learn the skills of time management
- Train people for notetaking
- Develop a critical sense
- Develop a spirituality that gives unity to life
- Make a personal option for Jesus Christ
- Create deeper bonds and promote an experience of church as community
- Develop a value system that gives direction to our lives
- Help people to move towards commitment
- Form leaders

Observation:
- The goals of the TCL should be previously written out on a poster and hung in a position where they can be easily read by all.
- The presentation of the objectives of the course should go beyond simply listing the above mentioned points. Appendix 8 indicates some suggestions for explaining the objectives. The facilitator should establish a link between these objectives and the participants' lives, by showing their importance for personal growth, for community building and for building a better world. The following are some examples:
    To be able to distinguish between values and counter-values is important in a world where there is a deep crisis of values. Self-knowledge is important if we are to correct our defects and take control for our lives. Without self-confidence, fear prevents us from taking on responsibilities. It is important to learn how to work as a team in a culture that educates us for individualism. Our commitment is stronger when it is motivated by faith. If we are to avoid being naïve people easily manipulated by the midia end unscrupulous persons we must develop critical sense. It is easier to understand the community of the followers of Jesus after having passed through an experience of community, during a course, than simply listening to many abstract talks on the subject. The formation of leaders is important because it is they have the capacity to train trainers and so involve the large mass of people.

d. How the Course Works

1. There are some possible misunderstandings we need to clear up at the beginning. This is not a course for listeners only. All are invited to participate. It is not a retreat or a course with many talks. It is rather a course with many different exercises and techniques for motivating the participation of all.
2. It is important to get to know one another in order to work well together. The success of the course will depend on the degree of participation of all.

3. The course is structured in such a way that continuous presence is necessary. Absence from a part of the course breaks the pedagogical sequence that links the different exercises into a global vision. Punctuality is also important to get the best out of the course.
4. Chairs are placed in a circle so that all can see one another without difficulty. The circle is a symbol of balance and equality where eye contact is possible and no one is in a position of prominence.

20.30-21.00 (30): Talk: Johary's Window (Appendix 9)
Facilitator: ....

Objective (Explain beforehand):
One of the facilitators explains the Johary's window exercise, making ample use of blackboard and explanation given in Appendix 9.

Maturity and depth of interpersonal relationships will depend on the capacity of those doing the course to increase the free area in their lives. The free area can be increased only to the extent that other areas are diminished.

The image of windows brings out the idea of being able see the others and others being able to see us. This is possible when we don't need to use masks. There is transparency between people. Our relationships are more authentic. We are freerer and we have control over the direction we will take in life. However, in order to increase these free areas we need to create an environment of confidence. This course aims at creating such a climate.

The explanation of the Johary's windows will be an important background support during the whole course. In different moments, different exercises will be used to widen the free areas in participants' lives and consequently reduce the other areas. In the explanation of these other exercises a reference can be made to Johary's Window and the need to widen the free areas in our lives, as a sort of thread that goes through the entire course.

Posters based on the drawing of Appendix 9 can be used by the speaker so that all can have a visual picture of the ideas being presented. The windows of the drawing can be covered and then uncovered as each window is explained. The challenge for the speaker is to illustrate the explanation of each window with concrete examples from daily life so the talk doesn't become too academic and disconnected from the concrete life situation of the participants.

21.00-21.30 (30): Distribution of Functions (Appendix 10)
Facilitator: ....

(a) Objective (Explain beforehand):
This exercise aims at forging the participants into a team. A facilitator explains that all groups have certain spontaneous social functions which frequently go unnoticed. These functions are fundamental for the development of true Christian community, team work and a more just and fraternal society. In the course these functions are institutionalised in order to train people for team work.

The speaker can ask the participants to think of a group, community or pastoral ministry that they know and where one or two people do everything. What is the difference when all 'pull their weight'? The example can also be used of a football team. Each player has a different function on a team. The team is successful when all 'work as a team'. It is important to link this exercise with the real situation lived by participants in their different groups and communities. How does your group or community work? Who participates? Who doesn't participate?

The Christian community should be a community of people, of believers, where all feel responsible and participate. We are all members of the same mystical body of Christ. Saint Paul states: 'There is diversity of gifts, but the same Spirit … while there are many members, there is only one body.' (1 Cor 12:5, 20) Our course can be an experience of community. Each one will have a different task to undertake in order to contribute to the common good of all. (These functions work well during the course. However, they should not be transferred mechanically to situations outside the course such as groups or community.) The general idea is that all should be involved in somehow contributing to the common good of the whole group.

The course will be an experience of the living out of values that contradict the consumer society in which in which we live where competition, appearances, profit, cunning and exploitation are the principal values (or counter-values). The different functions that people take on are different ways of serving the community.

Before applying the Exercise of Distribution of Functions, the following short exercise, called the Balloon Exercise, can be applied to help people discover the importance of teamwork and the division of tasks. It can also serve as an icebreaker. The facilitator asks for five volunteers and gives each a full balloon. The participants should throw their balloons high into the air without letting them fall to the ground. After a short time the facilitator asks one of the participants to leave the exercise. The remaining four have to keep the five balloons in the air. One by one the facilitator takes out the participants until there is only one left. He is unable to control the balloons on his own. The facilitator can then ask all the participants a number of questions: What they learned from this? Does this happen in your group? How can we improve this situation?

After this brief icebreaker the facilitator now applies the main exercise.

b. Application of Exercise (Distribution of Functions):
This exercise should be presented in the following sequence:

i) A very practical and rapid way of distributing the various functions is the following: Before explaining the objective, the sheet Appendix 10 is distributed to all, so that they can follow the explanation. The 13 possibilities should be written on the blackboard or on a poster, so that they can be seen by all. Beside each function is written the number of persons who can participate. The numbers written in the book presuppose that there are 26 participants. When there are fewer people, the facilitator should revise the distribution of numbers for each function and make the adaptations necessary.

ii) At the beginning of the explanation the participants are invited to begin thinking of the functions they would like to take on. It is good to have a number of options in mind, in case, later on, others take our first option.

iii) Different participants spontaneously volunteer to read aloud the text, describing the different functions. After reading each function the volunteer in question should explain it in his/her own words. The facilitator can clarify possible doubts.

iv) After the detailed explanation of the functions, all can approach the blackboard and write their names in the space that corresponds to the function they have chose. Care should de taken not to bypass the maximum number of people required for each function.

21.30-22.15 (45): Traffic Rules (Appendix 11)
Facilitator: ....

a. Objectives (Explain beforehand):
This exercise has as its goal to help the participants to learn the basic laws of group dynamics that facilitate team work and communication between people.

Norms and rules can often be oppressive and make life difficult. But, they can also facilitate our lives and our growth. It is important not to present the 'Traffic Rules' as something imposed from above, but rather as the essential values and relationships that have to be cultivated if we are to establish relationships, develop a community spirit and build a new society. To the extent that we work towards these new relationships we are already building a better world. The rules that we present here have as their aim to promote personal and group growth. We use the term 'Traffic Rules' because in traffic it is easy to perceive the importance of norms. Without norms, there is chaos.

The facilitator can ask the participants: If you go by car to a city and in the city each one drives according to his own whim as there are no traffic rules, what would be the result? Before reading the 'Traffic Rules', the facilitator can ask the participants to indicate some rules that would be important for the good functioning of a group or a community.

b. Explanation of Exercise
The facilitator applies the exercise in the following sequence of steps:
- He explains the aims of the exercise as we have outlined above.
- He then distributes a page with 16 rules (Appendix 11) for each participant.
- Each one reads the list silently and then turns it over on his or her lap. In this way the facilitator knows when the group as a whole is finished. Music can be played to help concentration.
- Each member is then asked to explain the rule that corresponds to the number on his nametag. Numbers above fourteen repeat the sequence 1, 2, 3… The faults noted in the interpretation of some of the rules should be corrected by the facilitator. In doing so, however, be careful not to discourage people by giving them the impression of not being intelligent.
- At the end of the explanation, the group decides the value of the fine for offences against the 'Traffic Rules'. It is recommended that the value of the fine should not be more than 5 or 10 cents – after all, the objective of the fine is pedagogical and not commercial. At the end of the course the whole group can decide on how to use the money collected from the fines.
- Starting now the Traffic Officer will take note of offences.
- Remind people that the collection of fines will take place during the presentation of functions on the following morning.

22.15-22.30 (15): Sociogramme I
Facilitator: ....

a. Objective (Should not be explained beforehand, without first of all helping the participants to discover for themselves through a short evaluation at the end of the exercise. Otherwise people do not learn to think for themselves.)

This exercise aims at measuring the relationships within the group: affinity, empathy, rejection, and difficulties between persons. The test takes an x-ray of the group and reveals important information which can be useful for building team spirit.

b. Application of the exercise

Slips of paper for voting (See Appendix 12) are given out with the following typed question:

'Who are the two persons I would like to work with in a group?'

1st choice_____

2nd choice_____

c. Explication
- It is important to explain well the whole voting process. A badly explained process can invalidate the results. Holding one of the voting slips in her hand the facilitator shows how to vote.
- Participants should vote only when the facilitator gives the sign. When voting only numbers, not names, should be used (As we have explained beforehand, when arriving for the course, each one should have received a nametag with his/her name and number.) . The numbers (on the nametag) of the persons chosen in first and second place should be written in the spaces indicated. After voting, each participant puts his/her own number on the back of the voting slip.
- It is important that each own knows the numbers of the others. Therefore the following step is important to avoid a situation in which the participants vote in a hurry without analysing all the options. The facilitator asks all to stand in a closed circle, so that it is possible to see the numbers of all. After each one has decided on the person to be voted, each one in sequence declares his/her number. People are now ready to vote.
- The two participants who are responsible for this exercise collect the voting papers. At the end of the day, one of the facilitators will show them how to calculate the results in the following way:
  - A large circle is drawn and the circumference divided by the number of people participating in the voting (the facilitators do not participate in the voting).
  - Draw arrows showing who voted for whom. The difference between first and second preference votes can be shown by using different colours or by using broken lines for second choices.
  - The names that received most votes for 1st and 2nd choices are printed at the bottom of the graph.
  - The graph is prepared by the two people responsible for this function and will be presented, during the presentation of functions, on Saturday morning.
  - The result of this first voting probably will not be very balanced, due to the presence of smaller sub-groups, which have not yet integrated themselves into the larger group. In the second Sociogramme a greater balance can be expected. On the other hand the third Sociogramme frequently shows a total imbalance, due to concentration of arrows on people who are reluctant to participate.

The graph on the next page, made out at one of the courses, visualises how to prepare the results.

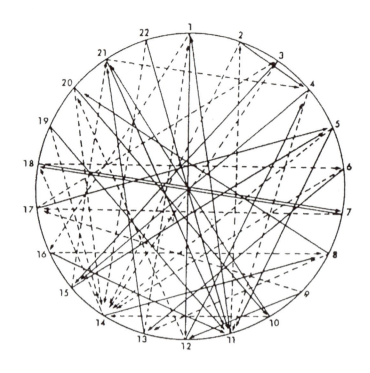

Results
_____ 1st option
- - - - - 2nd option

Results:
1st Choice: No. 11 received most votes (5 votes)
2nd Choice: No. 14 received most votes (7 votes)

22.30(05): Closing session
Facilitator responsible: ....

Some notices
- One of the facilitators reminds the participants about the time for starting and ending the sessions on the following day.
- Participants are reminded that one of the conditions for acceptance of candidates for the course was the possibility of being present at all sessions. The course follows a pedagogical sequence of themes and exercises and the absence from some of these can seriously harm the outcome.
- Tomorrow morning members should be prepared to present their functions. Half an hour has been reserved at the beginning of the morning session for the preparation. However, some participants have functions that demand more time for preparation. Therefore, these latter should start their preparation tonight or early tomorrow morning.
- Material being used should be left on the chairs. The Traffic Officer, however, may take home the Traffic Rules in order to study them better.
- The liturgical team should meet immediately after the closing session to prepare the Prayer Service for the following morning. The outline is ready (See Appendix 13). However, it is necessary to chose the hymn, the reflection psalm, the biblical reading, prepare the initial motivation and practice the 'Mantra'[1]. Those who have never

worked with a Mantra will need an explanation. Please consult the explanation given in the footnote. However, the best way of explaining a Mantra is to practice one. Choose a suitable refrain from a popular hymn and sing it as a Mantra.
- Since this will be the first more intense experience of prayer in the course, it is important that it be well prepared, since it will establish the spiritual tone for the remainder of the course. Some courses have shown that the members of the liturgical team lack confidence and experience. Its necessary to take into account the principle that 'nobody can give what he or she doesn't have'. One of the facilitators, therefore, should accompany the liturgy team, without creating dependencies or blunting initiative.

For this first prayer service, organised by the liturgical team, there is little opportunity for creating something different. There are motives for this. There is little time for preparation and the liturgical team, frequently, does not have much experience in this area. It is also the only moment of more intense prayer on the Saturday, so it is important that it be prepared well. On the other hand, on the Sunday morning the team will have liberty to create their own prayer service.

Due to the lack of time during the course, it is recommended that the final Celebration, on Sunday evening, be prepared during the preparatory meetings before the course by the co-ordination team itself (See Appendices 23A, 23B, 23C). Some of the participants can be invited to help with the less complicated functions in the celebration.

The Friday session closes with a spontaneous prayer.

---

1. A Mantra is the refrain of a hymn that is sung three or four times, each time lowering the volume, until finally it is sung in a humming tone, (with closed lips). When choosing the Mantra, the team should choose the refrain of a well-known hymn and should practice it beforehand with all those present. The Mantra helps the participants to concentrate their minds on God. In the Saturday morning Prayer Service (Appendix 13) the Mantra is the refrain from the psalm 'My shepherd is the Lord. Nothing indeed shall I want.' A different refrain can be used if this one is not known.

SATURDAY

08.45-9.15 (30): Morning prayer (Appendix 13)
09.15-9.45 (30): Free time to prepare functions

09.45-10.30 (45): Presentation of Functions
Facilitator responsible: ....

a. Objective (Explained beforehand)
This exercise aims at creating conditions for all the participants to work as a team, in which each one takes on a specific task. It aims at training the participants for teamwork, responsibility, community spirit and leadership. The facilitator comments: 'Yesterday we discovered ourselves and we discovered others. Today, by participating with different functions, we discover the importance of being at the service of others.'

The facilitator then passes the co-ordination of this session to the secretary who begins by reading a summary of the ideas and activities of the first part of the course. The secretary then calls each one in turn to present his/her function. Nobody should be left out. The order of functions on the sheet of paper can be followed.

Now and then, during the presentation, the facilitator may enquire if the tasks were done together as a team (i.e. when there are more than one person responsible for the function).

10.30-10.45 (15): Result of Sociogramme I
Facilitator: ....

Special attention should be given the presentation of the results of Sociogramme I. The facilitator who is responsible explains the objectives of the Sociogramme I: To take a photograph of the relationships between participants in the group and help the participants to understand the deeper group processes that they are normally unaware of. Attention can be called to the most voted and the less voted. The participants are then invited to evaluate and interpret the results.

The facilitator should be aware that this is a very delicate exercise. The persons who have not received any votes may feel upset. This exercise is necessary if we are to help participants to develop self-knowledge and widen the free areas in their lives. We can't make an omelette without breaking the egg. However, the debate should take place within a climate of understanding and care. The results are an alert for the participants who have not received any votes (they need to make a greater effort). It is also an alert for the others. The group as a whole should take care to bring into the group those who are on the margin. A mature group should integrate all is members and not only the friends, the extroverts, the good looking and the more talented.

10.45-11.00 (15): Coffee break

11.00-11.30 (30): Fishbowl Exercise Appendix 14A)
Facilitator Responsible.. + 1 assistant

a. Objectives (should not be explained beforehand, without first of all helping the participants to discover for themselves through a short evaluation at the end of the exercise. Otherwise people do not learn to think for themselves.)
1. To verify the level of competence of the participants in running meetings. To discover important rules for the correct functioning of a meeting or discussion group and errors that need to be corrected.
2. To connect the experience with what normally takes place in our groups, committees and communities. Do the same defects appear? Are our meetings usually better or worse?
3. To discover examples of bad communication and co-ordination ability that can be used during the talk on Group Dynamics that follows immediately. It is important, therefore, that the speaker should be present for this exercise.

b. Applying the exercise
1. The facilitator asks for eight volunteers and asks them to leave the room with the assistant facilitator.
2. Outside the room. The assistant facilitator explains that the members will form a Discussion Group. They will select a co-ordinator and choose one of the following topics. On returning to the room, the members will sit in the centre and will have 15 minutes to debate the topic chosen:
   - The death penalty is necessary to eliminate crime.
   - Young people should be allowed to drink in pubs at any age.

   The facilitator explains that the debate should be real and should not conducted as if it were theatre. The group should not practise the debate beforehand, otherwise it will not be spontaneous.
3. Meanwhile within the room:
   - While the Discussion Group is out of the room, the facilitator responsible distributes slips of paper with printed evaluation questions to those who have remained in the room (Appendix 14A). The questions to guide the evaluation should have been previously cut out with a scissors so that each member of the group receives only one question. Since there are only 15 questions, some questions will be repeated. Some questions will have two persons responsible. The facilitator explains that those who remained in the room constitute an Observation Group and their task will be to evaluate the debate that the group outside will conduct. He further explains that the members of the Discussion Group are not aware that they will be evaluated.
   - Chairs for the Discussion Group are placed in two parallel lines, in the centre of the room. The circle, as we have explained earlier, facilitates communication and the perception that all are equal. The chairs are arranged in this way to test the awareness of the participants of the Discussion Group of this important rule in communication.
4. When the members of the Discussion Group return to the room, they take their places. The facilitator gives the sign to begin the debate. During the 15 minutes debate, the members of the Observation Group remain in silence, observing the different aspects related to the questions they have received.
5. The facilitator indicates when the 15 minutes are up and asks the Discussion Group to

remain in the centre while the evaluation begins. Each members of the Observation Group reads his/her question and makes his/her evaluation. The members of the group in the centre are allowed to speak only after completing the evaluation. The aim of this rule is to avoid a tendency to defend oneself without first listening and being open to constructive criticism.

6. At the end of the evaluation, the facilitator asks the question: 'What have we learned with this exercise? Does anything similar happen in our communities, groups and schools?
Then the facilitator makes a general evaluation and explains the objectives of the exercise.
Observation: The evaluation is concerned with the skills involved in running a meeting – content is secondary. The more important aspects of this evaluation are: the skills for running a meeting or debate, the method used to make a deeper study of the topic discussed, the participation of the members and the skill of the co-ordinator to involve all members and help draw concrete conclusions.

11.30-11.45 (45): 1st Theme: Talk: 'Group Dynamics'.
Text of the talk + mini-dramas on different types of co-ordinators, (Appendix 14B, 14C)
Facilitator:...................................

a. Objective (Explained beforehand)
A member of the co-ordination team gives a talk on the importance of Group Dynamics (Appendix 14B). He explains the need for a clear understanding of some basic rules of group dynamics. Special importance is placed on the participation of members. Dialogue is presented as an important value: people must participate by communicating their ideas and, at the same time, learn to listen to what others are saying.

The use of posters, the blackboard or an overhead projector is important for visualising wrong and right ways of communicating. The previous Fishbowl Exercise (Appendix 14A) reveals the superficiality and lack of method in many of our meetings. Attention can be called to this. A short explanation of the See Judge Act Method is given at the end. The See Judge Act Method is an important instrument for arriving at a deeper understanding of the topics we study and also for developing a critical awareness. Due to the lack of time, the method should be studied, in greater depth, on another occasion.

During the talk the speaker organises four mini-dramas, of two minutes each, to illustrate the behaviour of four different types of co-ordinators. He asks for 5 volunteers for each sketch and indicates the co-ordinator of each. Each group is asked to simulate a meeting to organise an event in the parish or school to get funds for a group outing. The other participants are not aware that the four co-ordinators – one for each group – have been previously chosen and orientated to assume the behaviour of one of the four different types of co-ordinators: dictator, paternalist, *laissez faire* (permissive), and democratic (See Appendix 14C).

This talk is important to help participants understand the basic rules for working as a team.

11.45-12.30 (45): Exercise of Non Verbal Co-operation
Appendix 15A (Instructions for the group of observers)
Appendix 15B (Competitive situation/ co-operative situation)
(Envelopes with pieces of cardboard for forming rectangles)
Facilitator responsible: ……………………… + 1 assistant

a. Objective (should not be explained beforehand, without first of all helping the participants to discover for themselves through a short evaluation at the end of the exercise. Otherwise people do not learn to think for themselves.)

The aim of this exercise is to call the attention of the group to the fact that interdependence and co-operation are important human values and factors indispensable for team spirit and effective group action. In society and in the church people are accustomed to working with others using a the 'top-down' approach and not valuing people as responsible for their own formation and growth. The educationalist, Paulo Freire, talks about a 'banking education'. A top-down methodology is the basis for much of the authoritarianism, paternalism and individualism in our society. It is an ideology that undermines the possibility of teamwork, of building a mature Christian community and of building a more democratic and participatory society and church.

b. Application of exercise
Orientation for the co-ordination Team

It is important to check that the pieces of cardboard have been put back in their envelopes in the correct sequence after the last course. The pieces of cardboard should be prepared beforehand using the following schemes:

Contents of Envelopes:
- 1st Envelope: I – R – D
- 2nd Envelope: A – I – C
- 3rd Envelope: A – J – A
- 4th Envelope: D – E - C
- 5th Envelope: G – B – E
- 6th Envelope: A – C – D

1. The facilitator picks out twelve participants and divides them into two groups of six. These are called Groups of Collaborators. Each group is asked to sit around a table or on the ground at different ends of the room.

2. Twelve envelopes – 6 of one colour and 6 of another – have been prepared beforehand. The colours avoid the risk of mixing the two packs. Each group should have a pack of 6 envelopes of the same colour.

3. An envelope is placed in front of each member of the two Groups of Collaborators. Within each envelope there are three pieces of cardboard.

4. One of the facilitators explains that each member has five minutes to form a rectangle with three pieces of cardboard by exchanging his/her pieces with others. Rules that must be observed will be given out shortly. Please do not start until the sign is given.

5. At the same time as the two Groups of Collaborators are being formed, two assistant facilitators divide the rest of the participants into two other groups (Groups of Observers) and place each group standing around one of the Groups of Collaborators.

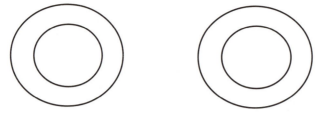

The members of each group of observers remain standing in a circle around its group of collaborators and position themselves in such a way that they can easily observe the behaviour of the group in the centre.

6. At the same time, the assistant facilitators distribute rapidly, and in silence, the evaluation questions for the groups of observers (Appendix 15A) – without the groups of collaborators being aware. The questions should have been cut out beforehand in slips of paper. Using sign language the facilitators indicate that each one should evaluate the group in the centre, based on the question received.

7. The facilitator, then reads the following instructions for the groups of collaborators and gives the sign to commence work on putting the rectangles together:

Instructions for the Groups of Collaborators
- Nobody is allowed to communicate either by word or gesture.
- Nobody is allowed to ask another person for a piece of cardboard.
- Members are only allowed to give pieces of cardboard to others.

8. When the exercise is finished the groups remain in the centre and the evaluation begins. The facilitator asks the members of the Observer Groups to evaluate the performance of the Groups of Collaborators. Questions are read out, one at a time, and answered by member of each group.

9. At the end the facilitator asks: 'What did we learn from this exercise? Some of the ideas that should emerge are: the problem of individualism (people who are only concerned with forming their own rectangle and don't think of helping others), the need for a co-ordinated plan in order to be more efficient, etc.

    If the group fails to form all the rectangles, the facilitator can show the correct way of putting the pieces together. At the end of the exercise the rectangles should be formed in the following way:

Finally the text *Competitive Situation, Co-operative Situation* (Appendix 15B) is distributed and two people, who read well, are asked to read it aloud.

12.30-12.40 (30): Sociogramme II
Facilitator Responsible: ....

To apply this exercise, verify the orientations for Sociogramme I. The graph with the results (in the form of a circular drawing) can be prepared during the interval after lunch.
The question to be answered: Who would I like to know better?
The result of this Sociogramme is presented after lunch.

12.40: Lunch
(Some courses avail of the lunch break to take a photograph of the group. Copies can be made available to those who wish to buy them at the end of the course.)

Exercise: 'Spirit of a Mule'
Facilitator: ....

a. Objective (Should not be explained beforehand, without first of all helping the participants to discover for themselves through a short evaluation at the end of the exercise. Otherwise people do not learn to think for themselves.)

This exercise aims at helping the participants to reflect on the many situations of conflict and oppression they meet with in daily life, the way they and the people around them normally react and the need to manage these situations in order to build a more fraternal human relationship between people. When we fail to administer these conflicts serious damage can be done to the work.

Conflicts are a part of life. We have to live out our faith in a society where conflict is present on all levels. Conflict can be an occasion of growth or destruction, depending on how we react to it on a psychological, political and faith level.

On a psychological level conflict between people is frequently caused by anguish, fear and insecurity. To the degree that we are supportive, people are frequently able to face up to their limitations and to some extent overcome them. On a political level conflict usually demands a much deeper structural analysis of the way society is organised and manipulated by economic interests.

b. Application of the Exercise
1. The organising team chooses one of the participants to start playing the role of the 'Spirit of a Mule' during the remainder of the course. The person selected is notified during the lunch break and, immediately when the course restarts, he begins to act in a way designed to irritate people. Only the organising team is aware that he has been oriented to act in this way. The person should be carefully selected, as this can be a difficult role to play. The co-ordination team should be on the look out for likely candidates during the first part of the course.
2. The facilitator will, later on, select the most opportune moment to reveal the role being played by the 'Spirit of a Mule', make an evaluation of the role played by the other participants in the conflictive situation and the different types of solutions attempted.

A link should be made to real life situations: group meetings, community living, political and social situations on local, national and international level. What are the causes and solutions for the situations presented by group? What are the consequences of an attitude of omission?

Observation: The use of this exercise requires a co-ordination team that has wide experience and is secure in itself. When in doubt, leave this exercise out.

14.00-14.45 (45): 2nd Talk: 'The Dignity of the Human Person' (See suggestions for the talk in Appendix 16A)
Facilitator Responsible: ....

a. *Objective* (Explain beforehand)

The 1st Theme, 'Group Dynamics', gave us important guidelines on how we should work together and what type of leadership we should be encouraging. This 2nd Theme is a key part of the course. The talk should aim at making each one aware of his/her dignity and the need to relate to others. Only in this way can each one grow as a fully human and happy person. The talk should give the theoretical basis for the experience that the participants are, in fact, living out together during the course. This reflection will be for many of the participants their greatest discovery: Each one is a person and for this reason has a special dignity and an enormous potential for growth. The bible establishes the religious basis for this dignity: we are sons and daughters of God.

The illustrations and concrete example used by the speaker are important to avoid giving an abstract and academic talk that fails to touch on people's lives.

Exercise: Before beginning the talk, the following exercise can be used to emphasise that each one of us is unique, with our own experiences and gifts. The participants are asked to close their eyes, relax and reflect on the answer to the question: 'If I were a chair, what type of a chair would I be?' The answers will normally be varied, depending on the very different experiences, desires and characteristics of each one.

14.45-15.15 (30): Result of the Sociogramme II
Facilitator: ....

a. *Objectives:*

This exercise helps the co-ordination team to analyse, on a deeper level, the interaction among the different members of the group.

Persons who received no votes are either already very friendly with the other members of the group or are being ignored by them. In the latter case the co-ordination team should try to detect the causes of this phenomenon and study ways of integrating them into a larger group.

b. *Application of the Exercise*

The Sociogramme is presented and attention is called to those who received the most votes and those who received the least. With regard to the latter no commentary is made. Care should be taken not to hurt those who received no votes. The facilitator should explain the importance of the exercise to help each one individually and the group as a whole to reflect on its behaviour. We can only grow as people, as authentic Christians and as community, to the extent that we face up to real situations, even though these, at times, may be painful. The participants can be asked to comment on the results.

15.15-16.00 (45): 3rd Theme: Jesus Christ (Study of text in group) (Appendix 17A)
Facilitator Responsible: ....

a. *Objective* (Should not be explained beforehand, without first of all helping the participants to discover for themselves through a short evaluation at the end of the exercise. Otherwise people do not learn to think for themselves.)

The text to be studied (Appendix 17A) continues the theme of the previous reflection on 'The Dignity of the Human Person' which dealt with the option we all face of choosing between the circle of death or the circle of life. People are enslaved by many counter-values. A Saviour is awaited. Christ appears in the lives of people as the messenger of God, as the Liberator who restores the necessary conditions for people to grow as persons. Christ is Liberator by his way of *'being'* (he is a person who loves deeply) and by his way of *acting* (he translates love into action by putting himself at the service of others, especially the poor and the abandoned).

A Christian is a person who has faith in Jesus Christ and is prepared to follow the path he has shown.

b. Application of exercise

The facilitator distributes the text to be studied (Appendix 17A) and orientates participants to meet spontaneously in groups of four persons. It is important to form groups with persons with whom we have had little contact during the course. The following are the steps to be taken:
a. Each group chooses a co-ordinator and a secretary.
b. The text is read and the group discusses the following questions:
    • What are the important ideas in this text?
    • What does Jesus Christ mean to me personally?

The principal ideas will be presented later in the plenary session.

16.00-16.30 (30): Coffee break

16.30-17.00 (30): Plenary Session
Facilitator Responsible: ....

a. Objective (Explain beforehand)
The Plenary Session should clear up any doubts that may remain about the text.

b. Application of the Exercise
Each secretary reports back the main ideas discussed in the small group. The facilitator makes a summary of these ideas on the black board and co-ordinates the discussion that follows. At the end, the facilitator summarises and complements where necessary. It is important not to remain only on the level of ideas. Faith for many is to a great extent intellectual and God is a distant God. An opportunity should be given for participants to talk about their personal faith in Jesus Christ.

17.00-17.15 (15): Sociogramme III (voting)
See Sociogramme I for orientations on his to apply this exercise.
Question for voting: Who are the two people who could have given more and didn't?

17.15-17.45 (30): Exercise: Preparation of mini-dramas (Appendix 17B)
a. *Objective* (Should not be explained beforehand, without first of all helping the participants to discover for themselves through a short evaluation at the end of the exercise. Otherwise people do not learn to think for themselves.)

This exercise aims at placing the participants in close contact with the Person of Jesus

Christ in the gospels. Jesus always acted in a conscious way, Seeing, Judging and then Acting.

b. *Application of exercise*

The facilitator responsible distributes Appendix 17B. It is important that each person has a bible. Participants are divided into five groups to analyse different biblical texts and prepare a small sketch of not more than 4 minutes. Suggestions for each group are given in the Appendix distributed. To avoid waste of time, the facilitator indicates the places for each group to meet.
- After reading the biblical text, the first 15 minutes are dedicated to a study of the question: 'What liberation does Christ bring us in this text?'
- A bell is then rung as a signal for the groups to start preparing the mini-dramas.

17.45-18.15 (30): Plenary of Mini-dramas
- Each group presents its mini-dramas without prior explanations.
- At the end of each presentation, one of the member explains the message the group sought to transmit and indicates the biblical text studied.

18.15-19.15 (60): Supper

19.15-20.45 (90?): Exercise: Psychological Profile (Appendixes 18A, 18B, 18C)

21. 20: Closing session: (Each group doing the Psychological Profile decides its own time for finishing

SUNDAY

08.45-09.00 (15): Morning Prayer
Facilitator: ....

09.00-09.45 (60): Presentation of functions
Facilitator: ....

At the end of this session the facilitator emphasises the importance of also taking on responsibility in one's group, community, school, and in society. 'No person is an island.' We are all responsible for one another as members of the mystical body of Christ.

09.45-10.30 (30): 4th Theme: Talk: 'The Church a Community of Brothers and Sisters' (See suggestions for talk in Appendix 19A, 19B, 19C)

a. *Objective* (Explain beforehand)
The talk on the church continues the ideas that were developed during the previous days (a link should be made with the two previous themes). The love proclaimed by Jesus Christ should lead to the living out of this love among his followers. The church is not the temple. It is rather the coming together of the followers of Jesus to carry on his mission.

The church has as its ideal the following of Christ: his example and his message. It should be a sign to the world of the love that unites her members: 'Love one another as I have loved you' (Jn 13:34). An early pagan writer in Rome wrote: 'See these Christians how they love one another.'

Christians are also open to the reality that is outside the church. In the wider society they seek to be the yeast that transforms. To be church means to be aware of the needs in the church community and also in the area where one lives and together with others do something to solve the social problems.

The church does not exist for itself. It exists to build the kingdom and is a sign of the kingdom. The kingdom is a wider concept than the church. This is why Catholics unite with other Christians and people of good will to promote the values of the kingdom: love, justice, fraternity, equality, and pardon.

10.30-11.00 (15): Coffee break

11.00-11.45 (30): Plenary Session: Debate on questions related to church and continuity.

11.45-12.15 (30 mins): Test: Time Management – Self Evaluation (Appendix 20A)

a. *Objective* (Explain beforehand)
The objective of this exercise is to bring each individual to an awareness his/her principal faults in managing time. The exercise is also a preparation for the talk that will follow on 'Techniques of Time Management'.

b. *Application of Exercise*
- The test is distributed to all the participants, who are requested not to read the text until instructed.

- Each one is asked to fill in the answers to the questions on the first page
- The facilitator then asks the participants to turn over the page and answer the questions on the second page.
- When all are finished the different styles of Time Management are read aloud.
- A debate follows using the following questions as a point of reference:
    1. What are my greatest difficulties for managing my time?
    2. What are the consequences for my lifestyle and my commitments?
    3. How can I solve some of these difficulties?

12.15-13.15 (60): Lunch

13.15-14.15: 5th Theme: Techniques of Time Management (Appendix 20B)

Objective

The study of the 1st theme, 'Group Dynamics], helped us discover ways of communicating better and being more effective in our work with others. The study of the 2nd theme, 'The Dignity of the Human Person', showed the potential we have for growth and the need to choose between a circle of life and a circle of death as we go through life. The study of the 3rd theme, 'Jesus Christ', puts us in contact with the person and message of Jesus and challenges us to embrace the same cause. Jesus' example and message are a concrete way of living out the circle of life. The study of the 4th theme, 'The Church as Community and a Sign of Service to the World', reminds us that the church is not the temple but rather the followers of Jesus who organise themselves to continue his mission over time. The study of the 5th theme, 'Techniques of Time Management', offers practical suggestions on how we can organise our time so that we can have a better quality of life and be more efficacious in our action. This is the theme we are going to talk about now. While this is not the more important theme, it is the issue that can block our capacity to translate our good intentions into action. Today we have less and less time. People's lives are cluttered up with so many unimportant things that many have no priorities in life. Time is an unrenewable resource. We need to learn to use well the time we have available.

14.15-14.30 (15): Exercise: Social Short-sightedness (Appendices 21A, 21B, 21C)
Facilitator: .... + assistant

a. *Objective* (Should not be explained beforehand, without first of all helping the participants to discover for themselves through a short evaluation at the end of the exercise. Otherwise people do not learn to think for themselves.)

This exercise aims at showing how people distort facts, make 'rash' judgements without thinking, how rumours arise, the difficulty people have in listening, the lack of a critical sense among the majority of persons and the facility in manipulating people who are not concerned with true facts.

The political dimensions of this exercise can also be explored: the way in which people are frequently manipulated by unscrupulous politicians, newspapers and television that present selected facts while ignoring others.

The physical surroundings can also be a hindrance to the transmission of a message (e.g. noise, temperature, etc.). In our courses it is important to create an environment that favours learning.

In our pastoral and social work it is important to give priority to written communication to avoid distortion of information and misunderstanding.

b. Application of Exercise
1. The assistant facilitator asks for five volunteers and takes them out of the room.
2. Within the room.
   - The facilitator shows a drawing, painting or overhead projection with a lot of detail to those who remain in the room. (See Appendix 21A) All should pay close attention and memorise the details of the drawing.
   - General Explanation. The facilitator explains what is going to happen. The members of the group outside the room will be called in, one by one. The first person called in will be shown a drawing and asked to pay close attention to the details. The drawing is then hidden, as it will be shown only to the first person.
   - Each time the second, third and fourth persons are called in, the observers should laugh out loudly to distract them (the group should not laugh when the first person enters, as it is important that he concentrate in order to memorise the details of the drawing – otherwise there will be little to be passed on). The facilitator will give an agreed sign to terminate the laughter. The same scene is repeated with the third, and the fourth person. As each new person enters the room the facilitator asks the previous person to tell him everything that happened since he entered the room.
   - At this stage the group of observers should not make any comments.
   - The idea of distracting with laughter is to show later on the importance of controlling outside interference if we want to communicate in an efficient way.
3. To begin: The first person is called into the room and asked to observe the drawing or painting in all its detail, as he will have to explain it to the next person who comes into the room. The observers remain silent.
4. The second person is called into the room (laughter and then silence). The first person is asked to describe what happened and what he saw after coming into the room. The second describes to the third, the third to the fourth and the fourth to the fifth. Only the first person will actually have seen the drawing.
5. Finally the facilitator presents the original drawing and conducts an evaluation of the experience by asking:
   - What did we learn from this exercise?
   - How can we apply to daily life what we have learned?
6. After the evaluation the text *Eclipse of the Sun* is distributed and read aloud (See Appendix 21B).

Observation: It is important that the first person called in has a keen sense of observation and is able to memorise well the details of the drawing before it begins to be distorted by the others. Overleaf is an example (there is another in Appendix 21A) of the type of illustration that can be used.

15.00-15.30 (30): Revision
Facilitator: ....

    The secretary presents a summary of the main ideas and activities of the second part of the course. The facilitator then makes a general review of the whole course and calls attentions to the objectives presented on the first day. These objectives can written on the blackboard or on a poster. The facilitator asks the participants to evaluate the degree to which the goals proposed at the beginning have been attained.

    Participants who were considered to have lacked participation in the last Sociogramme are given an opportunity to perform. They are given some very simple function to perform, such as the reading of some text, a poem or the explanation of an interesting saying. This is done in a light-hearted, humourous way.

    The last payment of fines is made and the group decides upon the destination of the money collected.

    The facilitator explains that the rules learned should continue being used after the course to deepen personal, community and social relationships. The external rules, used during the course, should now be interiorised in new behaviour patterns.

15.15-15.45 (30): Evaluation (Appendix 22)
Facilitator: ....

a. *Objective* (Explain beforehand)
    The evaluation is important for detecting the effect the encounter has had on the participants and discovering errors and ways of improving future courses.

b. *Explanation*
    The printed sheets with the questions for the evaluation are distributed (Appendix 22). Ten minutes are given to write out the answers to the question. The sheets are then taken up and the participants are given an opportunity to express themselves orally.

15.45-16.00 (15): Singing practice
16.00-17.00 (60): Eucharistic Celebration (Appendixes 23A, 23B, 23C)
17.00: Departure

PART 4

Appendices

Appendices: List of Materials for the Course

Appendix No 1A:	Weekend Timetable
Appendix No 1B:	Alternative Timetable
	Broken into Smaller Units (for night-time course, classes etc.)
Appendix No 1C:	Alternative Timetable
	Course Given during School Curriculum e.g. Module for Transition Year
	One day course
Appendix No 1D:	Two day course
Appendix No 1E:	Three day course
Appendix No. 2:	Form for preparatory meetings
Appendix No. 3:	Prayer to the Holy Spirit
Appendix No. 4:	General List of all Material Used in TCL
Appendix No. 5:	Form for indicating possible future facilitators
Appendix No. 6:	Explanation folder (for local community, school or other entity)
Appendix No. 7:	Model of Booking Form
Appendix No. 8:	Objectives of TCL
Appendix No. 9:	Johary's Window
Appendix No. 10:	Distribution of Functions
Appendix No. 11:	Traffic Rules (for better communication)
Appendix No. 12:	Voting papers for the Sociogramme
Appendix No. 13:	Morning Prayer (Saturday)
Appendix No. 14A:	Fish Bowl Exercise: Evaluation questions for the Observation Group
Appendix No. 14B:	1st Theme: Group Dynamics
Appendix No. 14C:	Instructions for the co-ordinators of the Mini-dramas (during the talk on Group Dynamics)
Appendix No. 15A:	Instructions for the Observers of the Non-verbal Co-operation exercise
	Envelopes with the cardboard pieces for the Non-verbal Co-operation exercise
Appendix No. 15B:	Text: Competitive Situation - Co-operative Situation
Appendix No. 16A:	2nd Theme: The Dignity of the Human Person
Appendix No. 17A:	3rd Theme: Jesus Christ
Appendix No. 17B:	Preparation of mini-dramas (biblical texts)
Appendix No. 18A:	Psychological Profile
Appendix No. 18B:	Personal notes
Appendix No. 18C:	Text: My beloved bamboo
Appendix No. 19A:	4th Theme: The Church as Community
Appendix No. 19B:	Text: The kingdom always lies beyond us
Appendix No. 19C:	Questions for discussion on continuity
Appendix No. 20A:	Time Management – self-evaluation
Appendix No. 20B:	5th Theme: Techniques of Time Management
Appendix No. 21A:	Picture for the Social Shortsightness exercise
Appendix No. 21B:	Text: The eclipse of the sun
Appendix No. 22:	Evaluation of the TCL
Appendix No. 23A:	Text: Celebration of Commitment
Appendix No. 23B:	Text of the 'Disciples on the Way to Emmaus'
Appendix No. 23C:	Functions for the Celebration of Commitment
Appendix No. 24:	Form for financial report
Appendix No. 25:	Model of badge as Symbol of Commitment
Appendix No. 26:	Model of nametag
Appendix No. 27:	Text: A Pastoral Experience: Using the TCL as a tool for renewal

Appendix No 1A:

Training Course for Leaders (TCL)

Timetable

Place: _____

Date: _____

Co-ordination Team:

Team Leader: ....
Members:
Member 1:.....................................
Member 2:.....................................
Member 3:.....................................

FRIDAY *Facilitator responsible*

19:30 (30)   Arrival, Reception, welcome, Nametags etc.   ___

20:00 (30)   Prayer and Introduction.
Presentation:
   The team and participants
   The objectives (Appendix 8)
   How the course works   ___

20.30 (30)   Johary's Window (Appendix 9)   ___

21.00 (30)   Distribution of Functions (Appendix 10)   ___

21.30 (45)   Traffic Rules (Appendix 11)   ___

22.15 (15)   Sociogramme I (Appendix 12)   ___

22.30 (05)   Closure   ___
Notices: Timetable for the following day, preparation of functions for the next session, importance of being present for the entire course, time for lights out, fines etc.

SATURDAY   *Facilitator*
                                                                            responsible

08.45 (30)   Morning Prayer (Appendix 13)   ___
09.15 (30)   Free time to finish preparation of functions
09.45 (45)   Presentation of functions   ___
10.30 (15)   Result of Sociogramme I   ___

10.45 (15)   Break

11.00 (30)   Exercise: Fish-bowl debate (Appendix 14A)   ___
11.30 (45)   1st Theme: Talk: 'Group Dynamics' (Appendices 14B, 14C)   ___
11.45 (45)   Exercise: Non-verbal Co-operation
                    (Appendices 15A & 15B)   ___
12.30 (10)   Sociogramme II (voting)   ___

12.40 ( )   Lunch: 'Spirit of a Mule' (optional)   ___

14.00 (45)   2nd Theme: Talk: 'Dignity of the Human Person'
                    (Appendix 16A)   ___
14.45 (30)   Result of Sociogramme II   ___
15.15 (45)   3rd Theme: Study of text & debate: 'Jesus Christ and
                    being a Christian' (Appendix 17A)   ___

16.00 (30)   Break

16.30 (30)   Plenary session   ___
                (The principal ideas of the groups should be written
                down on a blackboard and then a debate can follow)
17.00 (15)   Sociogramme III (voting)   ___
17.15 (30)   Preparation of mini-dramas   (Appendix 17B)
17.45 (30)   Plenary session   ___

18.15 (60)   Supper

19.15 (90?)   Psychological Profile (Appendices 18A, 18B, 18C)   ___
                Closure

SUNDAY   *Facilitator*
                                                                          responsible

08.45 (15)   Morning Prayer   ___

09.00 (45)   Presentation of functions   ___

09.45 (45)   4th Theme: Talk: 'Church as a Community
               of Believers' (Appendices 19A, 19B)   ___

10.30 (30)   Break

11.00 (45)   Plenary Session: Debate on questions related to church
               and continuity (Appendix 19C)   ___

11.45 (30)   Test: Time Management: Self Evaluation (Appendix 20A)   ___

12.15 (60)   Lunch

13.15 (60)   5th Theme: Techniques of Time Management (Appendix 20B)
               (improving the quality of your life
               and the efficacy of your action)   ___

14.15 (15)   Exercise: Social Shortsightedness
               (Appendices 21A, 21B, 21C)   ___

15.00 (30)   Revision   ___

15.15 (30)   Evaluation (Appendix 22)   ___

15.45 (15)   Singing Practice   ___

16.00 (90)   Celebration of commitment (Mass or Celebration of the Word)
               (Appendices 23A, 23B, 23C)   ___

17.30   Closure

Appendix No 1B:

Alternative Timetable
Broken into Smaller Units (for night-time course, classes etc.)

TIMETABLE

Place: _____

Date: _____

Co-ordination Team:

Team Leader: ....

Members:

Member 1:......................................

Member 2:......................................

Member 3:......................................

MONDAY

Facilitator responsible

19:30 (30)	Arrival, Reception, welcome, Nametags etc.	____
20:00 (30)	Prayer and Introduction.	
	Presentation of	____
	• the team and participants	
	• the objectives (Appendix 8)	
	• how the course works	
20.30 (30)	Johary's Window (Appendix 9)	____
21.00 (30)	Distribution of Functions (Appendix 10)	____
21.30 (45)	Traffic Rules (Appendix 11)	____
22.15 (15)	Sociogramme I (Appendix 12)	____
22.30 (05)	Closure	____

Notices: Timetable for the following day,
preparation of tasks, importance of being present for
the entire course, fines etc.)

TUESDAY

19:30 (30)	Arrival, snack	____
20.00 (30)	Morning Prayer (Appendix 13)	____
20.30 (45)	Presentation of tasks	____
21.15 (15)	Result of Sociogramme I	____
21.30 (30)	Exercise: Fish-bowl debate (Appendix 14A)	____
22.00 (15)	Break	
22.15 (45)	1st Theme: Talk: 'Group Dynamics' (Appendices 14B, 14C)	____
23.00	Closure	

WEDNESDAY   *Facilitator*
                                                                             responsible

19:30 (30)	Arrival, prayer	—
20.00 (45)	Exercise: Non-verbal Co-operation (Appendices 15A & 15B)	—
20.45 (45)	2nd Theme: Talk: 'Dignity of the Human Person' (Appendix 16A)	—
21.30 (15)	Break	
21.45 (30)	Debate	
22.15 (15)	Sociogramme II (voting)	—
22.30 (30)	Result of Sociogramme II	—
23.00	Closure	

THURSDAY

19:30 (30)   Arrival, prayer   —
20.00 (45)   3rd Theme: Study of text & debate: 'Jesus Christ and
             being a Christian' (Appendix 17A)   —
20.45 (30)   Plenary session   —
             (The principal ideas of the groups should be written
             down on a blackboard and then a debate can follow)
21.15 (30)   Break
21.45 (15)   Sociogramme III (voting)   —
22.00 (30)   Preparation of mini-dramas   (Appendix 17B)
22.30 (30)   Plenary session   —

23.00   Closure

FRIDAY

19:30 (30)   Arrival, prayer   —
20.00 (45)   Presentation of tasks   —
20.45 (45)   4th Theme: Talk: 'Church as a Community of Believers'
             (Appendices 19A, 19B, 19C)   —
21.30 (15)   Break
21.45 (30)   Plenary Session: Debate on questions related to Church and
             continuity (Appendix 19C)   —
22.15 (15)   Exercise: Social Short-sightness (Appendices 21A, 21B, 21C)   —
22.30 (15)   Revision   —
23.45 (15)   Singing Practice   —
23.30   Closure

SATURDAY

19:30 (30)   Arrival   —
20.00 (60)   Celebration of commitment (Mass or Celebration of the Word)
             (Appendices 23A, 23B, 23C)   —
21.00 (15)   Evaluation (Appendix 22)   —
21.15 (60)   Psychological Profile (Appendix 18A, 18B, 18C)   —
             Closure

Appendix No 1C:

Alternative Timetable
Course Given during School Curriculum e.g. Module for Transition Year

ONE DAY COURSE

TIMETABLE

Co-ordination Team

Team Leader:..

Members:

Member 1:..

Member 2:...

Member 3:...

Facilitator responsible

08.45 (15)	Arrival, Reception, welcome, Nametags etc.	—
09.00 (15)	Icebreakers	
09.10 (30)	Introduction. Presentation of • the team and participants • the objectives, • how the course works	—
09.45 (30)	Exercise: Fish-bowl debate (Appendix 14A)	—
10.15 (45)	1st Theme: Talk 'Group Dynamics' (Appendix 14B, 14C)	—
11.00 (15)	Break	
11.15 (45)	Exercise: Non-verbal Co-operation (Appendices 15A & 15B)	—
12.00 (45)	2nd Theme: Talk 'Dignity of the Human Person' (Appendix 16A)	—
12.45 (60)	Lunch	
13.45 (30)	Prayer (Appendix 13) – in an oratory or specially prepared environment.	—
14.15 (15)	Individual study: 3rd Theme: Study of text & debate: 'Jesus Christ and being a Christian' (Appendix 17A)	—
14.30 (30)	Study in Groups	
15.00 (45)	Plenary session (The principal ideas of the groups should be written down on a blackboard and then a debate can follow)	—
15.45	Written & Oral Evaluation – Closure	—

IMMEDIATE PREPARATION BY THE SCHOOL

The following list was made out for a school that gave the course to four transition year classes and may be helpful for other schools preparing to give the course.

1. Participants
- The 90 participants will be divided into three groups and the same course will be given to each group in three different classrooms by three different teams.
- Lists of the three different groups should be prepared beforehand and given to the co-ordination teams.
- Nametags should also be prepared beforehand, if possible in three different colours to distinguish the three groups.
- On the morning of the course an arrangement should be made by which on arrival the students are given their nametag and directed immediately to the classroom where their group will be meeting.

2. Preparation of three classrooms
- Desks should be taken out and chairs placed in a circle.
- Two table can be left in the room, one for material being used in the course and another for the speakers.
- Overhead projector in each classroom.
- Chalk, bluetack, markers and 8 large sheets of flip-chart paper.
- CD player.

3. Breaks
- For lunch sandwiches need to be prepared for the three teams giving the course.
- Tea or soft drinks should be made availabe at the tea-breaks in an area close to the classrooms. Perhaps an arrangement could be made to avoid long queques as the breaks are short.

4. Groups meetings
If possible an outside area close to the classrooms could be used for groups meetings in the afternoon.

Appendix No 1D:

Two Day Course

TIMETABLE

Place: _____

Date: _____

Co-ordination Team:

Team Leader: ....

Members:

Member 1:...................................

Member 2:...................................

Member 3:...................................

FIRST DAY   *Facilitator responsible*

08.45 (15)	Arrival, Reception, welcome, Nametags etc.	___
09.00 (30)	Prayer and Introduction. Presentation of	___
	• the team and participants	
	• the objectives (Appendix 8)	
	• how the course works	
	• icebreakers	
09.30 (30)	Johary's Window (Appendix 9)	___
10.00 (30)	Distribution of Functions (Appendix 10)	___
10.30 (45)	Traffic Rules (Appendix 11)	___
11.15 (15)	Break	
11.30 (15)	Sociogramme I (Appendix 12)	___
11.45 (30)	Exercise: Fish-bowl debate (Appendix 14A)	___
12.15 (30)	Debate	
12.45 (60)	Lunch Break	
13.45 (15)	Result of Sociogramme I	___
14.00 (45)	1st Theme: Talk: 'Group Dynamics' (Appendices 14B, 14C)	___
14.45 (45)	Exercise: Non-verbal Co-operation (Appendixes 15A & 15B)	___
15.30 (15)	Sociogramme II (voting)	___
16.00 (15)	Closure	___
	Notices: Timetable for the following day, preparation of functions, importance of being present for the entire course, fines etc.	

SECOND DAY

08.45 (30)	Morning Prayer (Appendix 13)	___
09.15 (30)	Half hour to prepare functions	___
09.45 (45)	Presentation of functions	___
10.30 (30)	Result of Sociogramme II	___
11.00 (15)	Break	
11.15 (45)	2nd Theme: Talk: 'Dignity of the Human Person' (Appendix 16A)	___
12.00 (45)	3rd Theme: Study of text & debate: 'Jesus Christ and being a Christian' (Appendix 17A) Study in Groups	___
12.45 (60)	Lunch	___
13.45 (30)	Plenary session (The principal ideas of the groups should be written down on a blackboard and then a debate can follow)	___ ___
14.15 (75)	Celebration of commitment (Eucharist or Celebration of the Word) (Appendices 23A, 23B, 23C)	___
15.30 (15)	Evaluation (Appendix 19)	___
15.15 (15)	Closure	

Return for night session???
19.15 (90)   Psychological Profile (Appendices 18A, 18B, 18C)   __

Appendix No 1E:

Three Day Course

TIMETABLE

Place: _____

Date: _____

Co-ordination Team:

Team Leader: ………………………………

Members:

Member 1:………………………………

Member 2:………………………………

Member 3:………………………………

FIRST DAY   *Facilitator responsible*

Time	Activity	
08.45 (15)	Arrival, Reception, welcome, Nametags etc.	___
09.00 (30)	Prayer and Introduction. Presentation of	___
	• the team and participants	
	• the objectives (Appendix 8)	
	• how the course works	
	• icebreakers	
09.30 (30)	Johary's Window (Appendix 9)	___
10.00 (30)	Distribution of Functions (Appendix 10)	___
10.30 (45)	Traffic Rules (Appendix 11)	___
11.15 (15)	Break	
11.30 (15)	Sociogramme I (Appendix 12)	___
11.45 (30)	Exercise: Fish-bowl debate (Appendix 14A)	___
12.15 (30)	Debate	
12.45 (60)	Lunch Break	
13.45 (15)	Result of Sociogramme I	___
14.00 (45)	1st Theme: Talk: 'Group Dynamics' (Appendices 14B, 14C)	___
14.45 (45)	Exercise: Non-verbal Co-operation (Appendices 15A & 15B)	___
15.30 (15)	Sociogramme II (voting)	___
16.00 (15)	Closure	___
	Notices: Timetable for the following day, preparation of functions, importance of being present for the entire course, fines etc.	

SECOND DAY   *Facilitator responsible*

08.45 (30)	Morning Prayer (Appendix 13)	___
09.15 (30)	Half hour to prepare functions	___
09.45 (45)	Presentation of functions	___
10.30 (30)	Result of Sociogramme II	___
11.00 (15)	Break	
11.15 (45)	2nd Theme: Talk: 'Dignity of the Human Person' (Appendix 16A)	___
12.00 (45)	3rd Theme: Study of text & debate: 'Jesus Christ and being a Christian' (Appendix 17A) Study in Groups	___
12.45 (60)	Lunch	
13.45 (30)	Plenary session (The principal ideas of the groups should be written down on a blackboard and then a debate can follow)	___
14.15 (30)	Preparation of mini-dramas (Appendix 17B)	___
14.45 (45)	Plenary session	___
15.30 (15)	Sociogramme III (voting)	___
16.45 (15)	Closure	

Return for night session???

19.15 (90)	Psychological Profile (Appendices 18A, 18B, 18C) Closure	___

THIRD DAY

08.45 (60)	Presentation of functions Result of Sociogramme III	___
09.45 (45)	4th Theme: Talk: 'Church as a Community of Believers' (Appendix 19A, 19B)	___
10.30 (30)	Plenary Session: Debate on questions related to Church and continuity	___
11.00 (15)	Break	
11.15 (30)	Test: Time Management – Self Evaluation (Appendix 20A)	___
11.45 (60)	5th Theme: Techniques of Time Management (Appendix 20B) (improving the quality of your life and the efficacy of your action)	___
12.45 (60)	Lunch	
13.45 (15)	Exercise: Social Short-sightness (Appendices 21A, 21B, 21C)	___
14.00 (15)	Revision	___
14.15 (15)	Evaluation (Appendix 22)	___
14.30 (15)	Singing Practice	___
14.45 (75)	Celebration of commitment (Mass or Celebration of the Word) (Appendices 23A, 23B, 23C)	___
16.00	Closure	

Appendix No. 2:

Form for Preparatory Meetings

Entity requesting the Course:_____

Date of Course:_____

Co-ordination Team:

Team Leader: _____
Members: _____
_____
_____
_____

PROGRAMMING OF PREPARATORY EVENTS	PERIOD	DATE	TIME
1. Definition of place, price, etc.	9 weeks beforehand		
2. Printing and distribution of Booking Forms	9 weeks beforehand		
3. 1st Training session of team/ distribution of functions	2 months beforehand		
4. Meeting with the local community & Logistics' Commission	7 weeks beforehand		
5. 2nd Training session of team	1 month beforehand		
6. Return of Booking Forms	3 weeks beforehand		
7. 3rd Training session of team	2 weeks beforehand		
8. 4th Meeting (when necessary): unfinished business	?		
9. Date for giving the Course			
10. Meeting for Evaluation & indication of future facilitators			

Appendix No. 3:

Prayer to the Holy Spirit

Facilitator: *Come Holy Spirit, fill the hearts of your faithful,
enkindle in them the fire of your love.
Send your Holy Spirit and everything will be created.*

All: *And renew the face of the earth.*

Facilitator: *O God who illuminates the hearts of your faithful
with the light of the Holy Spirit,
grant us that, in the same Spirit,
we may know what is right, and enjoy always your consolation.
Through our Lord Jesus Christ, in the unity of the Holy Spirit.
Amen.*

Appendix 4:

Materials used in TCL

Posters & transparencies
Church as Community
Dignity of the Human Person
Circles of Life and Death
Types of Co-ordinators
Techniques of Time Management
Forms of Communications
Material for Exercises & Talks
Johary's Window
Rectangles (packs with 6 envelopes)
Cards for controlling Time
Picture: Social Short-sightness
Paper titles: Objectives of TCL
Paper titles: Group Dynamics
Paper titles: Church as Community
Paper titles: D.Human Person
Paper titles: Time Management
Various
Pencils / Pencil sharpener
Rubber
Markers
Pens
Wooden ruler (30 cm)
Stapler (staples)
Cassette tape
Pritt (adhesive stick) & paper glue
Stapler (staples) & cello tape
String & wooden clothes pegs (hanging posters)
Folders
Typing paper
Poster paper & wrapping paper

Blue Tack
Chalk & eraser
Copied appendixes
Name-tags
Glue

Scissors
Pins
Old magazines
Overhead Projector

Celebration
Transparencies
Basket
Carpet
Symbol Commitment
Olive Oil
Fibre glass
Alcohol / Vases
Slips of paper

Tapes
Meditation

Books

TRAINING COURSE FOR LEADERS (TCL)
Place:_____
Date of Course:____/____/2_____
Co-ordinator: _____
Handed over by: _____
Returned+A207:___/___/_____

Appendix 5:

Form for Indicating Possible Future Facilitators
(at end of course)

GROUP OR ENTITY FOR WHICH THE COURSE WAS ORGANISED:

_____

PLACE: _____

DATE: _____

TEAM LEADER:_____

INDICATE POSSIBLE FACILITATORS WHO CAN BE TRAINED
AND INVITED TO PARTICIPATE WITH TEAMS GIVING FUTURE COURSES:

1. _____

2. _____

3. _____

4. _____

Appendix No. 6:

Explanation Folder
(for local community, school or other entity that has requested the course)

We have prepared this summary of the Training Course for Leaders (TCL) for the groups, community or schools that are thinking of promoting it.

The course has different advantages. It can be organised with only 4 or 5 facilitators. The cost is low. Motivation is strong as participants are not treated as passive listeners but rather are actively involved throughout the course.

The objectives of the TCL are:

- To help participants develop leadership skills. The exercises create learning situations that help members acquire the necessary skills for taking on the different leadership roles in the community, pastoral ministry, school or social environment.

- To acquire important skills for pastoral and social work: Serious preparation, personal organisation, team work, capacity to reflect and diagnosing the causes of the difficulties being faced, of searching for solutions and of guaranteeing continuity through personal and systematic follow up within a pastoral plan.

- To be a tool for involving parishes and schools. The TCL can serve as a tool to bring groups together and where there are isolated groups integrate them into a wider network. It can be a way of strengthening an organic pastoral ministry. For this purpose this course can be used with both young people and adults.

- To be a tool for involving young people. Young people who are not involved can be invited to take part in the course, and at the end, they are invited to be part of some type of organisational structure that guarantees continuity and where they can have ownership.

- Create deeper affective links among leaders on parish, school or diocesan level.

- Establish a link between faith and life. The course is based on five themes: Group Dynamics, the Dignity of the Human Person, Jesus Christ, The Church as Community and Techniques of Time Management. The different talks and exercises help the participants to link the Bible and doctrine to concrete situations in their daily lives.

- To transmit leaderships skills to the facilitators themselves. In each TCL course, the co-ordination team is composed of experienced and non-experienced facilitators. Each course has one or two new people who have previously done the course and have been invited back and trained to give the course to others. It's a strategy for multiplying leaders. Here, we follow an important pedagogical principal: the best way for a person to study a theme or learn a skill is to create a learning situation where he/she has to teach others. The skills and habits which the facilitators acquire as they prepare for the course will be automatically transferred to other pastoral situations: co-ordination meetings, meetings for planning, for evaluation, for organising different activities.

Preparation by the local community or school
The Local community, parish, school, diocese or organisation where the course takes place has an important role in organising the TCL. Its functions are:

1. Select 26 participants
   The pastoral ministry, movement or local community needs to define criteria for selecting the candidates for the course, discuss how to personally give out the Invitation Forms and how to guarantee the return of the forms together with the fee. A local person should be designated to be the contact person with the co-ordination team of the course. When the course is organised for participants from different communities or schools it is important that there be a contact person in each community who can easily be contacted by telephone, e-mail etc.

   When selecting the participants it is important also to include someone who has influence in the community or school and can help guarantee continuity afterwards.

   The course can be organised for young people, for adults or with a mixtures of both adults and youth. When the course is organised for young people, the presence of some adults facilitates greater dialogue, unity and co-operation afterwards, in the parish community or school. It can also be a way of involving adults who have a charisma and vocation for youth work.

   Where there are groups, the course can be used to strengthen them. Where there are no groups to guarantee continuity, the course can be used to form new groups or other forms of community experience. Participants are frequently highly motivated to think in terms of some form of continuity due to the bonds of friendship created during the course.

2. The financial question
   When participants have difficulties in paying the fee for the course, local leadership should organise some event to help: a dance, a raffle, a campaign to get food for the course, etc.

3. Time for arriving and leaving
   When participants return home at night time, it is important to establish the time for beginning and ending each day. This information should be on the Invitation Form that is distributed.

4. Distribution and return of the Invitation Forms together with the fee
   The candidates who have been chosen for the course need to be motivated and the Booking Forms need to be taken up on the date stipulated. Past experiences have shown that Team Leaders sometimes have fallen into the trap of simply giving out the forms as one of the many items referred to at the end of a meeting. The 'product' needs

to be marketed. The lack of marketing, explanation and motivation has sometimes meant that Booking Forms have not been returned in time and the course had to be cancelled. Today we live in a society where people's time is taken up with many invitations. We have to compete with other attractions and need to be able to show why our invitation is more important.

5. The Logistics' Commission
   The local community needs to pick a Logistics' Commission that is efficient, especially if meals have to be cooked and served by volunteer help. The responsibility of this commission will be to prepare the place of the course, be responsible for the cooking, transport and other tasks. The commission also needs to discuss the type of food and drink that will be served for lunch, supper and during the breaks. The kitchen staff needs to have a copy of the timetable to avoid delays. One of the facilitators on the co-ordination team should be the link person with the kitchen staff.

6. Transport home. When the course is organised on a 'sleeping at home' basis, it is necessary to foresee how participants are going to get home at night and return the following morning.

For more information please contact:

Appendix No. 7:

Model of Booking Form

TRAINING COURSE FOR LEADERS (TCL)

Invitation: We wish to welcome you to our next TRAINING COURSE FOR LEADERS (TCL) and are looking forward to and enjoyable and fruitful experience together.

Objectives: To train participants in skills for team work, self-knowledge, improving self confidence, interpersonal communications, time management, critical awareness, an experience of church as community, a spirituality that gives direction and unity to life, and leadership.

              For Further Information please communicate with:

The following is some useful information you need to keep in mind:
- Date: _____

- Time: Friday will begin at ....and finish at........................
             Saturday will begin at................. and finish at........................
             Sunday will begin at...................and finish at........................

- PLACE: _____

- FEE: Please return this Booking Form with the sum of _____

Booking forms can be returned to _____

OBSERVATION
- Due to the logical sequence of the course, only candidates who can remain for the entire period are accepted. Absence from any part of the course will mean the cancellation of your place.
- The fee covers all expenses, printed material, meals etc and should be returned with the registration form before the following date: _____
- Since there is a limited number of places available (26 places), we suggest that the registration form be returned promptly.

Take advantage of this unique opportunity. We are looking forward to meeting you and to having an enjoyable weekend together.

                                                              _____
                                                              General Co-ordinator

Registration Form
(to be returned)

TRAINING COURSE FOR LEADERS (TCL)

Please return this registration form to:

Name:	Birth date:
Address:	
City:	
Phone: Resid.:	Work:
Mobile:	E-mail:
Parish:	Diocese:
Are you involved in any voluntary activities in your school or parish? If yes, describe this activity:	
Study: Primary ( ) Secondary ( )	University ( )
Do you work? Yes ( ) No ( )	Profession
Civil state: Single ( ) Married ( )	
Have you participated before in any other encounter or course? If so what?	

Appendix No. 8:

Objectives of TCL

- *Train people for teamwork.* A popular saying reminds us that two heads are better than one. When we bring together our different talents and strengths we are more effective. Saint Paul points out that that we are all members of the same body, with different gifts that should be placed at the service of all. However, to work together we need to acquire the skills necessary for teamwork: skills for participating in meetings, for co-ordinating meetings and for working together.

- *Facilitate self-knowledge.* Self-knowledge is the key to developing one's personality. Many people rationalise their problems and project them on others. Without the capacity to recognise and correct our defects and errors we are incapable of growing and relating to others in a balanced and mature way. We become neurotic. We don't have our hands on the driving wheel of our lives. Conversion and growth in faith become impossible.

- *Build self-confidence.* One of the key discoveries of this century has been the discovery of the importance of self-esteem. Persons with low self-esteem are fearful of the future. They have no confidence in facing problems, nor do they inspire confidence in others. They are, therefore, not leaders. Self-esteem gives emotional security, diminishes anxiety, allows us to make important decisions calmly and to communicate positive thoughts to those around us. In this way we are able to help people to bond together and work towards a common ideal. Frequently, the difference between persons is not so much the problems they face as their attitude to the problems. And our attitudes are determined by our low or high self-esteem.

- *Acquire the skills for interpersonal communication.* Our happiness depends on our capacity to communicate with others. It depends on love, on friendship, on the ability to live in community rather than in an atmosphere of continuous hostility and bitterness. An effective pastoral organisation also depends on interpersonal communication. We need to eliminate emotional barriers and learn the basic rules of communication if we are to be fully realised and effective people.

- *Learn the skills of time management.* Today we have less and less time. People's lives are cluttered up with so many unimportant things that many have no priorities in life. We need to administer our time. We need to write down our commitments and decide on priorities. Many people complain of the accumulation of meetings. We often have to schedule an excessive number of meetings because we are inefficient in the way we run meetings. Sometimes we schedule several meetings to solve what could have been solved in one meeting or even outside a meeting.

- *Train people for notetaking.* Different studies have proven that immediately after a talk people remember very little of what they have heard. A week, a month, a year afterwards – much less. We need to acquire the habit of understanding and taking down ideas, otherwise we are unable to pass on the ideas to others. Neither will we have the capacity to argue in a coherent and logical way, to organise our ideas, to speak clearly. We remain intellectual weaklings.

- *Develop a critical sense.* A person with a critical sense is able to distinguish what is right and what is wrong, truth from half-truths. To have a critical sense means not to be a naïve person. It means having the capacity to think for oneself. The majority of people today unfortunately lack a critical sense. Many are guided by the opinions of others, by the TV, by the radio. Today, we have a generation that has been formed by the image and by constant stimulation that demand a tiny attention span. Most people today have little capacity to analyse different situations around them and to perceive deeper causes. They live in the present with little capacity to project themselves towards the future. They have learned to repeat, but not to create. Many reflect little before giving an opinion. Many are manipulated by unscrupulous persons for easy profit. This course proposes to revert this situation by forming people with a critical sense.

- *Develop a spirituality.* Spirituality gives a deeper meaning and unity to life. Many people today are discovering that material things do not answer their deeper existential needs. They are aware that there is something beyond themselves and that there is need for something that gives unity to life. Only spirituality can do that. Today, many artists talk openly about the place of spirituality in their lives. It is now 'cool' to talk about spirituality. The course helps to develop a spirituality that links faith and life.

- *Make a personal option for Jesus Christ.* Faith is more than a series of dogmas that we believe. Faith is especially a personal meeting with a person: the person of Jesus Christ. The New Testament reminds us that it was God who loved us first in the person of his Son. By accepting Jesus, we also embrace his plan for our personal lives and for society.

- *Create deeper bonds and promote an experience of church as community.* The course aims at making the course a community experience, an experience of a new style of church and a new society made up of 'new men and new women', to paraphrase St Paul's words. People acquire a sense of belonging to the church, not so much by listening to fine talks on the church but by participating in a meaningful community of faith.

- *Learn to distinguish between values and counter values.* Without the capacity to distinguish what is right and wrong a person has no direction in life. She has no reference points that give meaning to life. She has no compass. She becomes a person who is carried away with whatever wind is blowing. We live today in a society where enormous pluralism has led to fragmentation. There is a crisis of value. Many young people are confused and lost and have enormous difficulty in establishing their own identity. They find it difficult to find an ideal for which it is worth dedicating one's life.

- *Help people to move towards commitment.* We have a mission in the world, a mission received from God. The course has as one of its goals to help participants to take on some sort of concrete commitment in their community and in the surrounding social environment.

- *Form leaders.* To the extent that the course brings participants closer to the above goals, it is also forming leaders. This is a course for training leaders, agents of change, trainers of trainers. The leader is not born; he becomes a leader.

Appendix No. 9:

Johary's Window

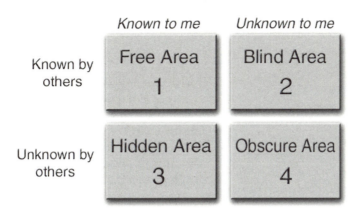

Explanation

1. *Free Area*

The free area of my personality covers my attitudes, behaviour, motivations and way of thinking, that are known to others and to me. When I have a large free area in my life, I can be transparent. For example, I don't say one thing and think another; I don't praise people to their faces and then undermine their character in secret.

It is the area in my life where I have no need to use masks. Real love and real friendship is only possible in the free area. The smaller the free area, the poorer and more superficial the relationships and the communication between people. The larger the area, the more free I am as a person, and the greater the capacity I have to develop authentic communication and relationships with others. This is where I am in contact with reality and avoid living in 'a fool's paradise'.

The reduction of other areas leads automatically to the increase of the free area.

2. *Blind Area*

The blind area covers my attitudes, behaviour, motivations and way of thinking that are known to others and unknown to me. It is the information my friends have about me but don't tell me; they are the impressions that others have of me, but for fear of my reaction, don't share with me.

Self-knowledge is the key to the formation of the human personality and for this reason I need the constructive criticism of others. I can only correct the shortcomings in my personality to the extent that I am aware they exist. If I have bad breath, for example, I can only correct the defect when a friend has the courage to tell me. If the impression that others have of me is that I am authoritarian, a snob, false, lazy, disorganised, irresponsible, cold, distant, that I hurt people with my attitudes – I can only face the problem and improve to the extent that I become aware of this reality. By refusing to allow others to tell me the truth I condemn myself to live in a world of illusions. We all build castles in the air. The problem is when we decide to live in them. Self-illusion eventually leads to stagnation and regression.

Self-knowledge is an important step in religious conversion. Jesus warned: 'How can you say to your brother, "Brother, let me take out the splinter that is in your eye", when you cannot see the plank in your own? Hypocrite! Take the plank out of your own eye first, and then you will see clearly enough to take out the splinter that is in your brother's eye.' (Lk 6:42). Where there is no freedom to speak openly, the atmosphere eventually becomes poisoned by suspicion, by lack of trust and by tension. Since problems are not faced or dealt with, they tend to get worse. We all know of groups and communities that have become stagnated on this level of communication. Friendship is no longer possible. A certain civility is maintained for appearances' sake. Confidence which is the basic ingredient for community growth has disappeared.

But, in order to accept the constructive criticism of others, I need to be able to run a risk, the risk of being rejected, of not being understood. I need to struggle against the temptation to flee, to attack, or to give people the 'silent treatment'.

3. *Hidden Area*

The hidden area of my personality covers my secrets. They are the attitudes, behaviour, motivations and way of being that are known to me, but unknown to others. My communication with others is authentic, real and profound to the extent that I am able to diminish this area. If a person refuses to open herself to me, I will have difficulty in knowing what her real sentiments and attitudes are. If I am secretly resentful of someone in the group, but never talk about it, it will be impossible to eliminate the barrier between us and solve misunderstandings and conflict.

Most of us have had the experience of someone confiding in us something very personal. Our reaction is usually one of feeling privileged (why me?) and honoured. Suddenly the distance between us disappears. The emotional links are strengthened. We became friends. Obviously, we are talking here of communication between emotionally balanced people.

This is the ideal situation. It doesn't mean, however, that I don't have the right to keep a certain number of secrets. Due to the limitations of our human situation, I need some masks to protect myself. However, the less the masks the freerer I am as a person and the more authentic and respected.

4. *Obscure Area*

The obscure area of my personality is the one which is unknown to others and, also to myself. It is the area of unconscious motivations, which sometimes have their origin in infancy. These exercise a strong influence over my attitudes, way of treating others, of seeing the world and of reacting in a certain circumstances. This is the area which is controlled by custom, social formation, fears, etc.

These unconscious motivations are similar to the large part of an iceberg that remains below the surface of the water. Only a small part appears above the water, the rest is submersed and we are never sure what is its real size. Similarly with our unconscious motivations, we are only aware of what we can see. Only psychological treatment can bring some of these motivations to the surface. Although unknown to us, these unconscious motivations continue exercising a powerful influence on our behaviour.

It is important to take into consideration this mysterious area of the human mind that exercises such enormous influence on our relationships with others and that, at times, is responsible for sudden outbursts and changes of behaviour. This self-knowledge makes us less likely to immediately put the blame on other people in conflictive situations.

Importance for our personal and group growth

The maturity of people and the depth of their interpersonal relationships depend on their capacity to widen the free area of their personality. The widening of this area happens when the other areas are diminished. A leader who has little capability to work on this free area, is incapable of motivating others on a long term basis

In general, the larger the free area, the better the quality of the interpersonal relationships. Our happiness and ideal in life depend on this. Friendship between two persons depends on this. Dating between two young people, also. It is difficult to establish a deep and stable relationships when the free area is small. A girl who married discovered that what was inside the beautiful package she had 'bought' was different from that which she had imagined. Living together in an intimate way, under the same roof, it was no longer possible to hide behind masks. After three months together the couple separated.

The use of the image of windows is especially important. A window symbolises a two-way communication. I can see the other person through a window and the other can see me. It means we need to use fewer masks. Our relationships can be more authentic. We are free and we have control over the direction of our lives. Now, to widen this free area an environment of confidence is necessary. At the beginning stage of a group or community experience, for example, the free area is normally small. To the extent that the level of confidence increases this area widens and the members of the group build more solid and deeper relationships. This course seeks to create this climate of confidence.

Interpersonal relationships and self-knowledge are important for building a Christian community. Grace builds on nature. Where there is neither self-knowledge, nor authentic human relationships, community becomes impossible. A community is not built only with ideas. The living out of the commandment 'love one another' must also involve us on the level of affections.

The explanation of the exercise 'Johary's Window' can serve as a background for the whole course. Many of the exercises during the course have as their aim the widening of this free area in our personalities and consequently the diminishing of the other areas.

Appendix No. 10:

Distribution of Functions

1) **SECRETARY (1 person)**
   The secretary takes notes of the sequence of activities and the main ideas discussed. For each activity he or she makes out a short report which is presented at the beginning of each day. He or she then co-ordinates the presentation of the other functions on Saturday and Sunday mornings by asking each one to present his/her different functions.

2) **TEAM FOR ORDER AND HOSPITALITY (3 persons)**
   The members of this team are responsible for making the other participants 'feel at home'. For this reason they should arrive before the others each day. They give out the name-tags at the beginning of the day and are also responsible for the smooth running of the course: keeping the place clean, checking the lighting, giving out material, music (record player), etc.

3) **TRAFFIC OFFICER (1 person)**
   There are the 16 basic rules (See Appendix 11) that are followed during the course. These rules facilitate teamwork and communication between people. A copy of the rules will be distributed later. The Traffic Officer is responsible for fining the offenders. He may take a copy of the rules home in order to study them (when participants go home at night-time) in order to pick out more easily the faults committed during the course. The price of the fine will be decided by the whole group and should not be such as to create an embarrassment for those who are in financial difficulties. We recommend that it should not be more than 5 or 10 cents. The fine is symbolic and is used for its pedagogical value.

4) **TREASURER (1 person)**
   During the presentation of functions, on Saturday and Sunday mornings, the Treasurer takes up the money for the fines as the Traffic Officer indicates the names of the offenders. At the end of the course the group will determine the destination of the money from the fines.

5) **ANIMATORS (2 persons)**
   The Animators are responsible for creating a lively, warm spirit in the group. During breaks they should encourage group singing, etc. Singing is important for creating an atmosphere that favours participation. Lively songs, linked with the themes of the day, are a special help. They may also use different games (that do not take up too much time).

6) **PSYCHOLOGISTS (2 persons)**
   The Psychologists observe the behaviour and personality of people during the course. In the session for presenting functions they can make an analysis of one or two of the other members or apply tests or psychological exercises on the group as a whole. In the case of tests, it is important to take into account the limitations of time.

7) **INTERVIEWERS (2 persons)**
   The Interviewers may ask one person two questions or two persons one question. The questions can be very simple and varied, according to be the environment and the person chosen: surname, profession, married or single, birthplace, family. More personal questions can also be asked: ideas and opinions on certain topics: education of children, dating, plans, etc. The interviewers should show concern for the person being interviewed and avoid causing any kind of shock which might cause her to close in on herself during the rest of the course.

8) **STIMULATORS (2 persons)**
   The Stimulators encourage the timid and give public praise to those who display qualities or talents that are important for community building. For this reason they are free to come in whenever they wish during the course. This function aims at attending to one of the deepest needs of the human heart: the need to be valued. Every human being needs to be valued. A pupil, for example, who is not accepted by his teacher, finds it very difficult to learn.

Acceptance does not mean that we ignore the defects of others or that we do not wish them to change. Modern psychology shows us that it is only when we accept the other person, as he or she is, that a person has the courage and strength to face up to defects and overcome them.

Lack of acceptance can lead to showing off, rigidity, inferiority complex, and the desire to dominate others and assert oneself. Saint Augustine wrote more than a thousand years ago: 'A friend is someone who knows everything about you and still accepts you.'

9) GOSSIPERS (2 persons)
The Gossipers aim at creating a happy environment by making up humorous gossip related to happening, facts and characteristics of members of the group.

10) 'CLIQUE-BREAKER' (1)
The Clique Breaker breaks up cliques by asking people to change places and reminding the Traffic Officer to fine the law breakers. His function is to help participants to mix and avoid remaining only with friends.

11) WALL NEWSPAPER (2 persons)
The people responsible for this function prepare posters with drawing and cutting to illustrate both serious and humorous aspects of the encounter. Use can be made of happenings and sayings in the group. However care should be taken not to offend people.
This exercises helps to create a happy and joyful atmosphere.

12) LITURGY (2 persons)
The members of this team are responsible for short prayer services, at the beginning and end of each day, and when they judge necessary during the course. The plan for the first prayer service is already prepared (See Appendix 13). Also, at the end of the last day, there is a Eucharistic Celebration of Commitment or a Celebration of the Word (See Appendix 23A) which has also been prepared beforehand. The co-ordination team is responsible for this latter celebration due to the lack of time during the course for preparing something completely new. This final celebration can be an important spiritual experience for the participants.

13) SOCIOGRAMME (2 persons)
Three times during the course there will be voting and the results will be calculated and presented in the form of a graph (Sociogramme). The two people responsible for the Sociogramme will conduct the different voting to evaluate the different types of relationships between those doing the course. The results are made out in graph form and presented to the group. (See the explanation of the sociogramme which follows). One of the facilitators will explain to the two persons responsible for the exercise how to prepare the graph.

Appendix No. 11:

Traffic Rules
(That make communication easy)

1. Meetings give best results when people sit around in a circle. In a circle all are equal. Nobody is in a position of prominence or domination and all can see each other. We can make eye contact.

2. Make a point of getting to know the persons you are less acquainted with. Give them the opportunity of knowing you. Don't form subgroups. Be involved with the wider group, talk frequently in terms of the 'we'. When speaking, speak to the group.

3. Be an active member. Look at the person talking. Listen. Don't talk in a low voice with your nearest companion. Value the ideas of others, especially when put forward by the more timid. You are on the team, so play. Take the ball and run with it when it's passed to you.

4. Don't make strong, absolute statements of rejection during the discussion (e.g. 'You are completely wrong!') This can create emotional barriers that make it difficult for the other person to keep the discussion on a rational level. Emotional barriers can close the doors to dialogue. Disagree in a more respectful way so as not to hurt or marginalise the other person. Use terms that will lead to consensus rather than confrontation.

5. To liven up the discussion, propose a contrary statement. Disagree. Demand proofs. In this way people are obliged to examine other perspectives and other angles of the questions in discussion.

6. If the meeting is going badly, propose a short evaluation. Don't wait for after the meeting to criticise. Be faithful and authentic.

7. The person who doesn't understand the topic being discussed is extremely necessary to the group. He asks basic questions that very often are not clear to the majority. Every group should have such a person. It is not a shame not to know.

8. Praise the good qualities of others. When a colleague says something that you agree with, make some a sign of acknowledgement. People grow when they are stimulated. Praise is like the sun for the plant: without it there is no growth. Praise stimulates greater involvement and creates unity.

9. When you intervene, always refer to some previous statement, even when you are disagreeing. This helps continuity. Don't make kangaroo jumps, ignoring the logical sequence of the discussion. Integrate your ideas with the ideas of others. A discussion should be a co-ordinated mental operation.

10. The role of the co-ordinator is of fundamental importance, especially for a new group. As the group matures, however, the co-ordinator's role becomes less important to the extent that the group as a whole takes on responsibilities. The co-ordinator should give opportunity to all to speak. The discussion should follow a sequence that leads to a deeper understanding of the theme. A co-ordinator who centralises decisions and responsibilities creates dependencies and is incapable of forming leaders. All the members are responsible for the group. Each member should feel just as responsible as the co-ordinator. There is no one owner of the group. All are owners.

11. When the discussion is very theoretical, demand facts to support the statements being made. Facts 'bring people down from the clouds' and make the discussion objective (inductive method or See-Judge-Act Method). Facts help to bridge the gap between faith and life.

12. Don't be preoccupied with the success of what you are going to say. Try not to justify yourself. Be yourself.

13. During the course, titles and professions should be ignored as they can create distance between people.

14. Each person should be called by his or her own name. Phrases such as 'you there' or 'that one there' or the one in the blue shirt, increase the distances and do not facilitate community building. Nametags should be worn at all times so that people will get to know one another by name. Addressing a person by name is one of the most important ways of showing appreciation.

15. Punctuality at the beginning of the day is a sign of seriousness and respect for others.

16. When the course is given in a retreat centre where participants are not required to return home at night time, the right of others to sleep should be respected.

Appendix No. 12:

Voting papers for the Sociogramme

The facilitator responsible for the three sociogrammes should prepare, beforehand, the voting papers with the following questions:

Sociogramme 1

Who would you like to know better?

1st option:_____

2nd option:_____

Sociogramme 2

Who are the two persons with whom I would like to work in group?

1st option:_____

2nd option:_____

Sociogramme 3

Who are the two persons who could have contributed more to the group and omitted to do so?

1st option:_____

2nd option:_____

Appendix No. 13:

Morning Prayer (Saturday)

1. Invitation to Prayer

2. Hymn (chosen by the liturgical commission)

3. Reading from the Bible (chosen by the liturgical commission)

4. Psalm and Mantra (seated)

   The Lord is my Shepherd (Psalm 23)
   Refrain sung as a Mantra (Each time softer and finally in a humming tone):
   My shepherd is the Lord. Nothing indeed shall I want.

   Spoken together:
   i. My shepherd is the Lord, there is nothing I shall want;
   Fresh and green are the pastures where he leads me.
      Mantra: My shepherd. .
   ii. The Lord gives me repose, close by waters cool and clear;
   And my soul shall be strengthened by his mercy.
      Mantra: My shepherd. .
   iii. He guides me on my way, on sure paths he sets my feet;
   For the Lord shall be faithful to his promise.
      Mantra: My shepherd. .
   iv. In darkness shall I walk, and in shadow lies my path;
   But no evil I fear for you are with me.
      Mantra: My shepherd. .
   v. Your shepherd's rod and staff shall be comfort on my way;
   For secure is the shelter that you give me.
      Mantra: My shepherd. .
   vi. A banquet you have spread, while in envy watch my foes;
   You anoint me with oil, my cup flows over.
      Mantra: My shepherd. .
   vii. Through all the days of life, only goodness follows me;
   I shall dwell in the house of God forever.
      Mantra: My shepherd. . .

5. Participants are invited to repeat spontaneously some phrases of the psalm that attracted their attention.

6. Spontaneous Prayers

Our Father, Hail Mary, Glory be to the Father.

Appendix No. 14A:

Fish Bowl Exercise:
Evaluation questions for the Observation Group
(Cut out and distribute the questions)

1. Was the meeting dynamic? Were the participants interested in the topic?
2. Did the participants listen carefully to the other members of the group or were they concerned only with preparing and defending their own ideas?
3. Was anyone unpleasant? Who appeared to be the friendliest?
4. Who was the most prominent? Was he/she positive or negative?
5. Was there a co-ordinator? Was the co-ordinator too domineering or did he get others to participate and take on responsibility in the group? Was he lost?
6. Was there agreement? Who agreed with everything and appeared not to have an opinion of her own?
7. Who was angry? Who was timid?
8. Who was hesitant about what she had to say?
9. How many times did each one speak?
   Did everyone participate?
   Who remained silent? Only listened?
10. Did anyone dominate the discussion?
    Who adopted an attitude of teaching?
    Who talked as if he were giving a class and the others were his pupils?
11. Did any member interrupt a colleague when speaking?
    Did he upset his colleague's explanation?
12. Was anyone left out in the group?
13. Were there cliques within the larger group?
    Were there several parallel discussions going on at the same time? Did anyone speak alone and was ignored by the others?
14. Was the discussion productive?
    Was there a conclusion?
    Was any method used in the discussion to guarantee a logical sequence of thought?
15. Did anyone have 'fixed ideas' and refuse to evolve?
16. Who failed to respect the different ideas of another member?

Appendix No. 14B:

1st Theme
Group Dynamics

As Christians we are called to live as conscious and responsible people, in a world of continuous change. Looking back on our lives we discover a continuous process of change. We are quite different people from some years ago. The world around us is continually changing and as a result new questions and new problems emerge. Alone we feel very vulnerable in a rapidly changing world. We are frequently incapable of facing many of these problems on our own, or giving answers to the questions that trouble us. We need others; we need to work together. And one of the fundamental tools for working together is dialogue. Dialogue is in fact one of the important values needed in the modern world. However, dialogue presupposes that we have learned the skills necessary for working in groups.

Almost everything we do in the church and in society, we do in groups. The importance of small groups is not a new discovery. Over two thousand years ago Jesus Christ used a small group of twelve people as his principal strategy for spreading his message to the four corners of the world.

We live in groups but, frequently, we don't know how to work in groups. We don't know how to work in a team. Society trains us for individualism. We frequently commit errors because we lack guidelines and preparation for working together. This is where Group Dynamics can help us. Group Dynamics is a branch of the Social Sciences that teaches us the techniques and the rules for working together, for analysing our problems, for discovering the best solutions and how to move from 'goodwill' to 'concrete action'. The Traffic Rules that we have studied, for example, are one aspect of group dynamics.

1. Objectives of Group Dynamics
Group Dynamics can help people:
a) To seek together the solution for the problems they face. The information that others have and their way of looking at the problem can help us to find more rapidly the solution to the difficulties and issues we face.

b) To make possible growth in group and in community. This presupposes that all are interested in the same problems and have similar objectives. The group will grow only to the extent that all the members participate.

c) To seek a real dialogue in which all members participate as equals, contributing with his or her particular talents and outlook.

2. Rules for Group Dynamics
Group Dynamics points to two basic rules for those who want to work as a team: the need to present your ideas and listening to the ideas of others.

a) Present your ideas
- Organise your ideas before speaking. Some people speak without thinking. The basic rule is: 'Before putting your lips in motion, turn on your mind.' A person who has not learned to organise her ideas is confused and is incapable of convincing others.
- Speak openly on the proposed topic. Give opinions, but in doing so relate them to the opinions of others.
- Speak, inspiring and creating an atmosphere of confidence. The basic attitude of each participant should be one of respect for the other person, even when there is disagreement on the level of ideas.
- Speak, without monopolising the time available for others:
  - don't interrupt
  - don't be false by pretending to be in agreement. Always be authentic;
  - don't form cliques.

b) Listening
You should be concerned to:
- Listen to what the other person has to say and not only to what you would like to hear. We often have a selective filter… we ignore that which questions us and does not support our own ideas. We think our idea is the only unique idea of value; we anxiously wait for the other to stop talking so that we can expound on our own idea. We don't listen because we are not interested in what the other has to day. We are involved in a dialogue of deaf people. With this approach there is no possibility of growth – neither personal growth or growth as a group.
- Listen and try to understand objectively, without prejudice against the person who speaks (sympathy or aversion);
- Listen calmly in order to understand better. Don't be worried exclusively with what you are going to say or answer (otherwise you are not really listening).
- Help the more timid members to express themselves. Their contribution is equally important.
- Improve communication between people.

3. Examples of wrong types of communications in group dynamics
There are a number of forms of communication between people that are prejudicial to personal growth and growth as a group. The following drawing visualises these negative forms of communication:

   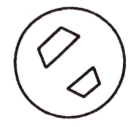

Monologue   **Giving a class**   **Crossed dialogue**   **Isolated subgroups**

The correct way of communicating should involve everybody in both the discussion and search for solutions to the problems we face. This approach can be represented visually as a spiral which diminishes as it approaches the centre or conclusion:

True dialogue

The spiral symbolises debate which begins by analysing as much relevant information as possible. The See Judge Act method helps us to avoid dispersal of ideas and organise the discussion so that we arrive at a deeper understanding of the topic discussed and draw conclusions that can involve members in concrete actions.

4. Types of Coordinators
In all social groups the co-ordinator is a key figure and catalyst of the individual energies. We should, therefore, give special attention to the leaders when we wish to create, modify or improve a gathering of people, be it a community, an association, group or class at school. Care should be taken in the way these leaders are selected or elected and also in the way they are trained.

The co-ordinator will have qualities that are above the average in his group and be able to transmit new knowledge to other members. In this sense the co-ordinator is an educator.

But nobody is born a leader; rather he/she can become a leader. We can discover potential leaders and help them develop leadership skills. For this reason we need to distinguish between the type of leader that promotes new leaders and the types who prevent the growth of leadership.

We present some of these types of co-ordinators in the following pages. The explanation of each type can be preceded by a mini-drama according to the instructions in Appendix 14C.

a) Dictatorial Co-ordinator

The dictatorial co-ordinator is not interested in knowing what his or her 'subordinates' think. He refuses to accept any type of questioning. Anyone who questions is seen as bad, as an enemy. All the members of the group depend exclusively on the 'dictator', who has the maximum authority. The members are there to carry out orders.

a. Do what I tell you!

Sometimes the dictatorial group may appear to be democratic. In fact, subtle means are employed to guarantee the execution of all orders that emanate from above.

Frequently, this type of co-ordinator is repeating a type of formation received in childhood. Attitudes of previous educators are reproduced. On the one hand, he may be the product of an authoritarian background or, on the other hand, he may have been exclusively spoiled as a child and allowed to dominate those around him, including his parents.

In this type of group, the members usually grow apathetic and lose a spirit of initiative and responsibility. The environment can be one of strong emotional pressures. Sometimes a type of guerrilla warfare emerges between members: some in favour of the authoritarian leader and others making a strike for freedom.

Depending on the qualities of the authoritarian leader, dictatorial groups often give the appearance of being more efficient in carrying out decisions. Eventually, however, these groups break up or become prisoners of formalism.

b) Paternalistic Co-ordinator

a. Leave it to me, I'll do

In this case the leader is seen as 'good' and represents the 'father' or 'mother' figure. Everybody depends on his 'advice'. He gives the impression of having the good of the group at heart.

Emotional dependency is increased. A love-hate feeling develops as the members become aware of the need to strengthen their own personality and to take initiative.

The paternalist leader reproduces the same situation as a dictatorial group. In fact, the negative consequences are probably greater as he creates emotional dependence. It is more difficult for members to rebel, to affirm their own personality and right to think for themselves. The members are afraid to hurt this type of co-ordinator by criticising his behaviour, because 'after all he is so good and selfless in sacrificing himself for others'.

c) Permissive or 'laissez-faire' Co-ordinator

You know yourself.
Do whatever you think best!

Laissez-faire, in French, means, 'letting do'. The motto of this type of co-ordinator is to do nothing in the hope that the problems and challenges will go away.

In general this type of co-ordinator is a very insecure person, who is fearful of taking on responsibility.

Unlike the dictatorial co-ordinator, who is accustomed only to giving orders, the Laissez-faire or Permissive leader doesn't give any orientation at all. Each of the members of his group 'does his own thing, when it comes to dividing out work and responsibilities', there is a total confusion. His lack of leadership causes dissension and disorganisation among the members. They remain together because of friendship or out of some vague desire to achieve a common objective. Due to the frustration provoked by the lack of direction and achievement, these groups usually disappear or become dictatorial groups in order to survive.

d) Democratic Co-ordinator

Ok! We're all in this together!

The democratic co-ordinator believes that it is easier to solve problems with the help of the group rather than working on his own. While the paternalist co-ordinator does the work of ten people, the democratic co-ordinator motivates ten people to become involved. He or she respects the members and believes in them. He gets the co-operation of the group by his competence, patience, tolerance, honesty and sincerity of his proposals. He doesn't give orders, he gives example and encourages, rather than reprimands. He aims at making people think for themselves. He gets the results by creating a climate of goodwill.

All are involved in the common activities and have clear idea of the objectives of the group. There is a free exchange of ideas and open discussion on the most efficient ways of acting. Solutions are not imposed, but worked out together.

Unfortunately, many co-ordinators are afraid of losing their status as new leaders come to the forefront. Not so the democratic leader. He encourages constructive criticism. The members are aware of their responsibility in striving towards a common goal. The co-ordinator perceives the natural leaders as they emerge progressively in the group and forms them for leadership. His model is that of John the Baptist, whose aim was to diminish so that others could grow.

5. Develop a critical sense
The function of group discussion is to form the members into leaders who are able to analyse critically the daily occurrences around them and to become involved in the building of a better world. To develop a critical sense, in today's society, means having the capacity to distinguish truth from untruth, to weigh arguments and not allow oneself to be manipulated by others. A young person recently put it this way: 'To develop a critical sense is to is to refuse to be a fool, controlled and manipulated by others.'

Unfortunately, the majority of people lack critical sense, are indifferent, alienated and easily manipulated. They accept blindly statements made by the mass media and by unscrupulous people in positions of power, without attempting to verify their truthfulness.

A reporter in London interviewed Dr Albert Schweitzer, winner of the Nobel Peace prize in 1962: 'Doctor, tell us, what is the worst defect of modern man?' After a short silence, he answered: 'Very simple. People today don't think.' Robert Main, the famous American psychiatrist, in his book *Man in Search of Himself*, states: 'The contrary value in today's society is not cowardice but rather conformity.'

We have here one of the main problems of our times: conformity and the inability to think for oneself. The majority of people follow the crowd; young people may bow to peer pressure without knowing why or what they want, nor how to go about attaining their goals. We live in a world where there are few authentic leaders. This course is a step in the direction of changing that.

6. The See-Judge-Act Method
The Vatican Council recommends the use of the See-Judge-Act Method to form Christian leaders. 'Formation for the apostolate cannot consist only in theoretical instruction. Lay people must learn gradually and prudently, from the beginning of their formation, See-

Judge-Act, always in the light of faith, to form and improve themselves and others through action, and in this way, enter into the active service of the church' (*Decree on the Apostolate of the Laity*, Chap VI, No 29). The following is a brief description of how the method works:

B) SEE (Survey of the reality)

i) At the beginning, facts, problems or issues from real life situations are presented. The decision is then taken on the aspect of the issue that will be discussed. It is important to limit the theme at this stage otherwise so many different topics will be brought into the debate and any in-depth discussion will be impossible.
Examples of Facts: In the local pub someone made the following statements:
- 'The poor are poor because they are lazy.'
- 'The death penalty is the best way of diminishing crime.'

ii) Analysis of the facts presented
- Care should be taken not to remain in a theoretical discussion which fails to touch on the real life situations. Demand facts.
- To what extent are the facts presented mere rumours opinions. The first attitude may be one of distrust of the fact or facts presented.
- Universal aspect: Is it an isolated fact or is the issue presented here universal?
- See the fact as part of a complex whole. Are there other facts that could give a clearer picture?

iii) Causes
Without looking at and dealing with causes there are no lasting solutions to the problems we face. Sciences such as Sociology, Economy and Psychology can help us understand deeper causes.

iv) Consequences
The experiences of each one are important to get a deeper understanding of the topic under discussion. Those who have less experience participate by asking questions.

Having studied the facts we can now judge them.
B) JUDGE
The facts, happenings, opinions, etc, related to the problem, are judged in the light of the group's principles – the principles that should guide the search for lasting solutions. For Christians, these principles are contained in God's revelation through the person of Jesus Christ. We find this revelation in the Bible and in the church documents.

Revelation should give the profound and ultimate meaning to the problem that has been studied in the first part of the meeting (SEE). In the second part of the discussion (JUDGE), we look at the different events and situations through the eyes of faith.

For this reason, it is important that our mentality be impregnated with the gospel. In the gospels we not only come in touch with the teachings of Christ but also meet him directly as a person, ask him what he did, what he said, to illuminate in this way the present situation.

The same Christ is present, today, in the concrete situations of our lives.

We meet together 'in the name of Jesus Christ' and are therefore aware of the special presence of the Lord in our group: 'Where two or three are gathered together in my name I am in the midst of them' (Mt 18:20).

C) ACT
The discussion should lead to concrete suggestions for action.

Here we answer the call of Jesus to personal conversion, to involvement in our community and to transform unjust social structures in our society. This is the most important part of the meeting. If the discussion does not lead to action we are largely ineffective as a group. St James reminds us that 'faith without action is dead'.

D) 'RE-SEE' (SEE AGAIN)
It is important to have another look, in the following meeting, at the decisions taken. A competent co-ordinator should demand accountability for decisions taken. Demanding systematic accountability creates a climate of seriousness and responsibility. Evaluation of action leads the members of the group to learn lessons from their mistakes and become encouraged by their successes and victories.

Appendix No. 14C:

Instructions for the co-ordinators of the Mini-dramas
(during the talk on Group Dynamics)

A. ORIENTATIONS FOR THE FACILITATOR OF THE EXERCISE

This exercise involves two different moments:
before and after the talk.

1. Before the talk
During the course, the facilitator who gives the talk
on 'Group Dynamics' should choose 4 people to act out the roles of the four different types of co-ordinators: dictatorial, paternalist, permissive and democratic. These can be chosen either from the co-ordination team or from the participants in the course. This sheet is given to each one of the four, who in turn pick the type of co-ordinator that they wish to act out. The speaker should meet with the four persons beforehand to discuss how they will represent the different types of co-ordinators and be clear on the exact moment that each one will enter. It is important to write the names of the four people involved beside the type of co-ordinator they will represent. This can avoid last minute misunderstanding and confusion.

2. During the talk
Before speaking on the dictatorial co-ordinator, the speaker asks for 5 volunteers to present a brief mini-drama of 2 minutes on how to organise a dance in the parish to get funds for a particular church activity. The person chosen to play the role of the dictatorial co-ordinator should present himself/herself spontaneously, as one of the volunteers, and is then indicated by the speaker to co-ordinate the group during the mini-drama. The other participants are not aware that the co-ordinators have received instructions on how to behave. When the mini-drama is finished, the speaker asks the participants to indicate the type of co-ordinator represented and, then, talks about the dictatorial co-ordinator, illustrating his talk with examples taken from the mini-drama.

Before speaking about the other types of co-ordinators, the speaker uses the same strategy. As each group of volunteers presents itself, the co-ordinators who have been previously chosen, in secret, present themselves as volunteers, following the order on this sheet: dictatorial, paternalist, permissive, democratic. In all, four mini-dramas of two minutes each are presented, each dealing with a different type of co-ordinator.

B. ORIENTATIONS FOR THE COORDINATORS OF THE MINI-DRAMAS

The following are some orientations to help the people previously chosen for the roles of different types of co-ordinators. Each one can reflect beforehand on what type of behaviour best corresponds to his/her role.

1. Dictatorial co-ordinator
The group organises a meeting to plan an event in the parish or school to get funds for a group outing. You have two minutes to co-ordinate the meeting as if you were a dictatorial co-ordinator who doesn't care how his subordinates think. The other people in the course don't know that you have been chosen beforehand for this role.

2. Paternalist co-ordinator
The group organises a meeting to plan an event in the parish or school to get funds for a group outing. You have two minutes to co-ordinate the meeting as if you were a paternalist co-ordinator who believes in centralising everything and doesn't delegate. The other people in the course don't know that you have been chosen beforehand for this role.

3. Permissive co-ordinator
The group organises a meeting to plan an event in the parish or school to get funds for a group outing. You have two minutes to co-ordinate the meeting as if you were a permissive co-ordinator who doesn't who takes no initiative and gives no direction to the group. The other people in the course don't know that you have been chosen beforehand for this role.

4. Democratic co-ordinator
The group organises a meeting to plan an event in the parish or school to get funds for a group outing. You have two minutes to co-ordinate the meeting as if you were a democratic co-ordinator who believes in working together as a team. The other people in the course don't know that you have been chosen beforehand for this role.

Appendix No. 15A:

Instructions for the Observers of the Non-verbal Co-operation exercise
(Cut out and distribute to the observers)

Each of the Observers Group receives a written slip of paper with the following questions:

POINTS TO OBSERVE

1. Who offered some of his pieces of cardboard to others?

2. Did anyone manage to put together his/her rectangle while in the process of separating himself/herself from the rest of the group?

3. Did anyone try tenaciously to put together his rectangle, while ignoring his or her colleagues?

4. How many really become involved in trying to form a rectangle?

5. Who are the members of the group who became anxious or frustrated because they failed to form their rectangle?

6. Was there a critical moment in which the members of the group really started to co-operate?

7. Who tried to break the rules of the game?

Appendix No. 15B:

Text: Competitive Situation – Co-operative Situation

COMPETITIVE SITUATION	COOPERATIVE SITUATION

COMPETITIVE SITUATION

1. People think only of themselves.
2. People consider others as adversaries and adopt unscrupulous methods to keep them down.
3. People try to hide their real ideas and feelings from their 'adversaries'.
4. People try to confuse the discussion so that a conclusion becomes impossible.
5. People try to increase rivalry among others by spreading gossip and distrust.
6. People use any and every means, even dishonest ones, to impose their ideas.

COOPERATIVE SITUATION

1. People are preoccupied with their colleagues.
2. People build sincere friendships with others.
3. People present their ideas in a sincere and frank way.
4. People help the group to strengthen the bonds of unity among the members.
5. People avoid gossip and work together in an atmosphere of trust.
6. People make an effort to listen to the opinions of others. The ideas of others are respected and valued and all the members work towards a group conclusion, where there are no losers and winners.

Appendix No. 16:

2nd Theme:
The Dignity of the Human Person

1. The Human Person is born with enormous potential for growth
The human person, at birth, appears to have very little that makes him or her different from animals. The child doesn't in any way behave like a human being. It seems to reacts only to stimuli from outside. Nevertheless, it is very different from the non-rational as it has the potential for becoming a fully human person who can hope, create, discover, reflect, take on responsibility, participate, grow as a person, learn, feel, reason, adapt herself to her environment and, principally, *love*.

Each human being is born with possibilities for growth: possibilities for observing, judging and deciding before acting. The human person can choose between different options. She can refuse to be controlled by instincts. She is not programmed like the animals. In this way she is very different from animals, whose reactions are determined by instinctive behaviour. A person who acts instinctively, without observing, judging and deciding is less a person, is not free, is not in charge of herself, and is incapable of real happiness. She remains on the level of the animal. She is programmed like a computer. Because she acts like a robot she is incapable of true happiness as a human being.

In order to grow as persons and develop the different possibilities and horizons that are open to us, we need to be aware and reflect on the following:

2. You are a unique being
You are a unique being. In all creation, only you can think and choose between different options. This uniqueness is also a result of a decision made by God himself. You were chosen from all eternity to be a son/daughter of his. The Bible reminds us that it was God who took the initiative. He loved you first.

One of the key discoveries of this century has been the discovery of the importance of self-esteem. Persons with low self-esteem are fearful of the future. They have no confidence in facing problems, nor do they inspire confidence in others. They are, therefore, not leaders. Self-esteem gives emotional security, diminishes anxiety, allows us to make important decisions calmly and to communicate positive thoughts to those around us. In this way we are able to help people to bond together and work towards a common ideal. Frequently, the difference between persons is not so much the problems they face as their attitude to the problems. And our attitudes are determined by our low or high self-esteem.

Therefore, the most important investment is needed in people's self-esteem. This is also true for social transformation, for those who are marginalised by society. We need to repair weakened confidence if we are to empower people and help them to grow and break the vicious circle of poverty.

So you are a unique being. You can make decisions, you have your own gifts, capabilities, preferences, your own way of looking at things and situations. In the midst of billions of human beings in the world there is no other person the same as you. You were not factory-created, on an assembly line. As God created each one of us, he threw out the mould. The uniqueness of each individual brings a great richness to the relationship between people. We need each one as he or she is. Each one has different gifts. Difference is not a threat; it is a richness. When we work in a team, we complete one another. It would be a sad and monotonous world if all of us were clones of one another.

Uniqueness does not mean separation from others but, rather, an enriching of the relationship between people. The human person is created for others; he or she is a social being.

3. You are a social being
When a person wishes to live isolated from others, it is usually a sign of abnormal behaviour. Because we are social beings, we need others and others need us. That is the way we were manufactured. We live in constant contact with others. It is exactly through this relationship that we grow and develop as persons. We need to be in constant interchange with others in order to grow emotionally, intellectually and spiritually.

Our first community was the family into which we were born. From the family we moved into the wider community (neighbourhood, school, work) where our growing and maturation process continued. To grow we need others. Much of the rich qualities of our personalities are the result of the self-giving of others. Many of the things we use daily were made for us by others. Almost everything we know we learned from others.

To the extent we dedicate our talents to serving others, we help them to grow as individuals and members of a community. We ourselves also grow at the same time. That is why everyone has a responsibility or task in this course. The parable of the Talents reminds us that God has given us different talents – talents we should develop and place at the service of others. 'Who is my neighbour?' is the question presented by Jesus. To answer the question he had formulated, he told us a story, the story of the Good Samaritan.
Our attitude of service, however, should be a conscious one. It should lead people to take on responsibility for their own destiny by developing a critical awareness: the capacity to See, to Judge and to Decide, before Acting.

The values lived in this type of relationship are very important: love, justice, liberty, health, education, fraternity, recreation, peace, etc.

4. To be a fully mature person means having a hierarchy of values
In the first book of the Bible we are told that the human person is called by God to take charge and develop the world. His vocation is to become a conscious person (who thinks, judges and decides before acting). Many people today, however, do not think for themselves, are manipulated, live their lives around a few superficial and shallow goals. There is no hierarchy of values in their lives. Their goals are often limited to their next purchase. The call of the Creator to widen their horizons and embrace a cause that really gives a deeper meaning to life goes largely unheard.

Within a post-modern culture there is a crisis of values. The principal concern is with the present, with feeling good, with sensations of the moment. There is a rejection of universal values. Values are seen as subjective. The attitude of many people is one of: 'What is right and wrong depends on how I feel.' The demands of love and solidarity are not taken into account. And so life can becomes very superficial. We are talking here of a culture of pleasure. Pleasure, which in itself can be a good thing, becomes the absolute value, the value for judging all other values. There is no longer right and wrong. Everything is valid if it makes me feel good. Within this worldview, the suffering caused to other people is not taken into account.

But without a value system we have no direction in life. We are on the high seas in the midst of a tempest without a map or a rudder in our hands. A person with a conscience knows that not everything has the same value, the same weight. There are essential values and values that are passing. There are values and principles that we can never sacrifice under any pretext. We can't speak of Christianity, of faith, of spirituality without speaking of a hierarchy of values. There has to be a hierarchy of values in life, in order to judge situations around us and to have control and direction in life. The gospel helps us establish this hierarchy of values.

A conscious person knows that he is at a crossroads and has to choose between two roads: between a road that gives priority to values and a road that gives priority to countervalues. He has to choose between a circle of life and a circle of death. He has to choose the road less travelled and that will make all the difference.

A person who lives consciously is capable of thinking and judging the more important values that should be present in a relationship with other people. He is capable of discovering those essential values which are: love, justice, liberty, truth, etc. In a world that is continually changing these remain as permanent values.

Transitory values are also important. They can help us to live the essential values. Some of these transitory values are: technology, money, leisure, pleasure, etc. However, when we place these transitory values at the centre of our lives, then we upset the hierarchy of values. Here we have the root cause of many of the major problems in the world today. Much of the poverty in the world today, for example, is caused by an economic system that considers only profit and economic efficiency while leaving out the impact on the quality of life of the wider population.

5. Challenge: To choose between two options

We were born as a being with potential,
with many possibilities:

- To Think-Judge-Act
- To learn
- To discover new ways
- To choose between different options
- To develop oneself and to grow
- To love and be loved
- To share and live in community
- To transform our environment
- To communicate with the Creator

However, we can choose not to develop these possibilities. We can choose another path. Because, in life we are faced with two options. We can choose:
a)   The circle of life or
c)   The circle of death

When we have a correct hierarchy of values then we are strengthening the circle of life. When the hierarchy is inverted then we are strengthening the circle of death.

a) Circle of life
We know that God loves us and desires our happiness. He has placed certain dynamic forces within us which, when put into practice, build the circle of life and, consequently, our dream of happiness. God wants us to take charge of our own destiny and not simply be objects, manipulated by others.

We can present this *Circle of Life* in the following way:

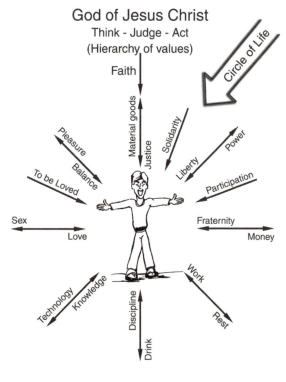

Lack of respect for this hierarchy of values harms our relationship with others and leads to discord (for example: to prefer money to justice, vice to health, sex to a relationship based on love and respect, etc). So we need to reflect on the following questions:

- Does the environment we live in create conditions for helping us develop as fully human persons? The parable of the Sower calls attention to the importance of the environment we create. There are environments that favour human and Christian growth and there are others that choke the fragile plant that is born.

- In the environment we live in, is there a predominance of such values as love, justice, liberty, fraternity or is the type of relationship between people largely determined by counter values?

- Are people being helped to develop their capabilities for thinking, judging, deciding and acting? Or are others deciding for them?

b) The Circle of Death

However, there is another option in life: the option for the circle of death. Many people choose or find themselves caught up in the circle of death.

The circle of death prevents the growth of the human possibilities God has given us. It is the circle of crime, violence, injustice, hatred, sickness, misery oppression, torture, vice, etc. This we call sin.

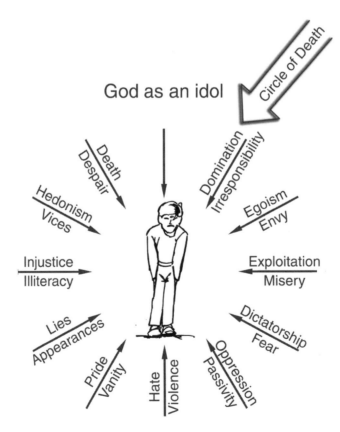

That is why St Paul describes sin in terms of slavery and death (cf Rom 6:23, 7:14).

In the circle of death there is an inversion of values, which prevents people from developing the gifts given by the Creator. In this circle there are people who put profit above solidarity and the dignity of the human person and as a result millions of children are affected, especially in developing countries. If we could shrink the earth's population to a village of 100 people, with all the existing rations remaining the same, it would look something like the following:
- 6 people would possess 59% of the entire world's wealth and all
- 6 would be from the United States
- 80 would be in substandard housing
- 70 would be unable to read
- 50 would suffer from malnutrition
- 1 (yes, only 1) would have a college education
- 1 would own a computer.

Children are born into these surroundings with little or no possibility of overcoming obstacles and having a dignified life. An analysis of the lives of many young people who populate the prisons in these countries reveal the influence of the surrounding environment on their growth: dysfunctional families, violence and drugs.

Sex is an energy that comes from the Creator and, therefore, is important for humanity. Some people, however, place sex above love and respect. Many young people discover, often too late, that sex, which was made for communion, can also lead to loneliness, to domination, to falsehood, to manipulation and to alienation. Sex which is separated from love and commitment has contributed to the increase of divorce, violence, rape and rejection. Sex without responsibility can mean a death sentence. Promiscuity today is an almost certain path to AIDS.

In the circle of death, there is a lack harmony between people. Unity and growth are not possible So, we need to work together to break this circle of death which is within us and also in social structures in society around us. For this we need to establish life-giving spaces where we can cultivate alternative values, otherwise the materialism and individualism of the surrounding culture engulf us. We need to make our contribution to the building and the strengthening of a circle of life in the society around us.

c) How can we Build the Circle of Life?
The construction of the Circle of Life will depend of two things:
   i) Conversion from personal sin and
   ii) Conversion from structural sin.

i) Conversion from personal sin
The gospel calls us to conversion, to change our lives, to change from selfishness to love, from a spirit of individualism to a spirit of solidarity. If we don't come to terms and learn to deal with some issues such as desire for revenge, anger, selfishness, resentment, fear, dishonesty and hypocrisy, it will be difficult to know God who loves us. Neither will it be possible to contribute to strengthening our community and building a better world.

ii) Conversion from structural sin
It is important to take into consideration that the establishment of a correct hierarchy of

values – and therefore the circle of life – does not depend only on the good or bad will of people. The way society is organised – the relationship between work and capital, the way of producing and sharing the good and distributing power – conditions people and largely determines the values that predominate in society. In religious language we refer to this situation as social or structural sin. Social structures, 'necessary in themselves, tend frequently to become fixed and hardened in mechanisms that are relatively independent of human will, paralysing or perverting in this way the social development and generating injustice.'

This unjust way of organising society, in order to favour privileged classes means that the majority of the population can never grow as human beings, because the lack the minimum of physical and material conditions.

The challenge is to articulate the concerns and problems of daily life: family conflicts, negative self image, unemployment of a family member, a father who is an alcoholic, friendship, profession, religion, leisure, personal problems … with the larger questions, on national and international levels: political, economic and social. Social analysis, which gives us a more scientific view of the 'inner workings' of society, is an important issue which we need to study in greater depth, in future courses.

6. Summary

In summary, we can say that individuals grow as persons to the extent that they relate, in a balanced way, to those around them and, in doing so, develop the capacity to See, Judge and Decide before Acting. The observance of a hierarchy of values will lead to a strong emphasis on love and justice which are the two values that determine the quality of a mature relationship necessary for building a New World.

As Christians we have the duty to fight against this wrong ordering of values, which prevents full human growth as unique individuals and as people created by God to complement one another in community. We need to join hands to break through this Circle of Death. A South African biblical theologian, Albert Nolan, has stated that the Old Testament can be summed up in one word: *Justice*, and the New Testament in another word: *Love*. It's not a bad formula for moving forward with improving our own lives and that of others.

It means choosing the Circle of Life over the Circle of Death. The aim of our church and social groups should be to create and strengthen the Circle of Life so that the word of God can grow and produce fruit. This is the vocation we have received from God. And we shouldn't be content with short, low flights when Christ has called to soar to higher things. Christ has broken the Circle of Death and revealed to us new horizons of hope. This leads us to our next theme: Jesus Christ.

Appendix No. 17A:

3rd Theme: Jesus Christ

In the previous talk on *The Dignity of the Human Person*, we talked about the negative reality of countervalues that form a Circle of Death around us. These countervalues not only prevent the growth of the human person, but also threaten to destroy him. There is a strong desire for freedom. A church document has pointed out that the 'The awareness of liberty and the dignity of man, conjugated with the affirmation of the inalienable rights of the person and of peoples, is one of the predominant characteristics of our time. However, liberty demands certain conditions in the economic, social, political and cultural order that make it possible to exercise it fully.' The Circle of Death not only holds back people's development but also threatens them with destruction. From the beginning of time people have lived with the anguish of not being able to overcome this Circle of Death and so have looked to a Saviour.

1. Freedom from the Circle of Death and countervalues
A man emerges in history who corresponds perfectly to this hope of salvation. His name is Jesus (God saves), Christ (the Anointed One). This man comes from God. He is the revelation of God. He is the Son of God. His mission is to save and liberate men and women, to give them conditions to free themselves from the Circle of Death, from the surrounding countervalues of egoism, envy, falsehood, war, violence, vice, fear, discord, poverty, hunger and ignorance. Jesus reveals that the plan of the Father is that love should be the force that bonds us together, in the concrete situations of our lives.

Being a Christian, therefore, means believing in Jesus Christ and accepting him as a model for our own lives. Christ's love gives us the power to change our lives. His message of liberation inspires us to work towards a more just and fraternal society which can be reflection of God's love for us.

2. Christ liberates, by changing different situations in life
Christ mixes with the people of his time, feels for them and participates in their problems. Let's have a closer look at how Jesus acts. This is not merely a story, a fairy tale. It is Christ who presents himself as he really is. A human Christ, fully a person, who uses his talents and qualities to make love possible between people. For this reason he is moved by the suffering of others, participates in their problems and seeks to solve them.

Let's have a look at the situation of the 'widow of Naim' (Lk 7:11-17). A funeral is being accompanied by a large crowd of people. A dusty road, many people with sad faces. The dead person was a boy, the only son of the widow. She cries. Her pain is great due to the loss of her only son. She has now been left alone in this world.

Christ, accompanied by his disciples and a large crowd, takes in the situation (is interested, reflects, judges), goes to meet the woman (makes a decision and then acts) and gently says to her: 'Don't cry.'

The words of Christ are very strong. They seem not to take the situation into account. How can she not cry? Nevertheless these are the words of Christ: 'Don't cry.' He consoles her, showing that he is not indifferent to her problem. In fact he has already become part of her life. And when he says, 'Don't cry,' it is because he will in fact transform her pain into joy.

Christ shows how much he is capable of loving: he gives back life to the boy! His words of consolation are now turned into reality.

The love of Christ brings about a total transformation in the life of the widow. Love transforms and changes a negative situation to a positive one. Christ's love goes so far as to change death to life.

The love of Christ is not a love of nice words, but rather a concrete love, which faces up to the challenge of transforming negative situations around him. He develops authentic relationships with others, shows interest in them, listening attentively; he is understanding in his attitude, communicates a message of love and hope and has a ready disposition for helping all those that cross his path.

3. Christ liberates by giving the person another chance and encouraging a change in life-style
Christ always involves himself with the people he meets. More than anybody else, he is convinced of the dignity of each person. He accepts people as they are, while giving them another chance.

We read in Jn 8:1-11 the story of the woman who was caught in the act of adultery and brought before Jesus by the scribes and the Pharisees. According to the law, she should be stoned to death. Nevertheless they want to know what Jesus thinks.

Christ turns the situation over in his mind. He knows that the Law is the maximum value for the Scribes. The maximum value for him is love and the dignity of the human person! He looks thoughtfully at the adulterous woman and then at the scribes. He judges the situation of both. All need liberation:
- for the scribes and the Pharisees: liberation from a Law that enslaves them.
- for the adulterous Woman: liberation from a wrong understanding of love.

The scribes and the Pharisees insist. Christ speaks. He decides to act: 'One of you who is faultless shall throw the first stone.' Just that.

The attitude of Christ and his way of putting the problem make the scribes and the Pharisees reflect on their own lives. They *judge* that they are also sinners, that their way of acting is not correct, even though it be within the Law. Here they have to make an option: choose the way of being and acting of Christ, which means accepting love as the maximum value, or to continue acting as they have always done: judging others by the Law without taking into account the human circumstances and refusing to give people another chance! The scribes and the Pharisees leave, one by one (they See, Judge and then Act), starting with the eldest. Jesus remains alone with the woman. He then turns to the woman: 'Where are they? Has no one condemned you?' Christ's attitude towards her accusers makes the woman reflect on and judge her own life, which was certainly not flawless. Her answer is full of hope and, at the same time, anguish. She is fearful: 'Will he condemn me or give me another chance?' In her, 'Nobody, Lord,' is contained her sincere goodwill to start all over again. Jesus says to her. 'Neither do I condemn you. Go and sin no more.' He is able to see the good that is present in her life. 'Go and learn to really love.'

Christ involves himself in the lives of the scribes and the Pharisees and the adulterous woman, in order to change their way of life. He helps the former to discover that love is above the Law; that the dignity of the human person has to be the centre of our preoccupations. He helps the woman to break out from the circle of her egoism, isolation and marginalisation, in order to love truly.

4. Christ liberates by his way of being
The values of a fully realised person are to be found in the life of Jesus Christ. He is not a prisoner of his instinct. He *Sees, Judges* and then *Acts* when faced with different situations. He is a free person: free of selfishness and social pressure (the 'common sense' of the Pharisees, fear, etc.). His originality and freedom endows him with special authority and attracts people to him. He is the ideal of a fully realised person.

5. Christ liberates by his way of acting
As a self-realised person, Jesus is totally open to others and mixes with them; he makes deep friendships; he creates conditions for love by eliminating barriers that separate people. He combats the countervalues (injustice, disunity, violence, formalism, falsehood, oppression, misery, hunger, ignorance, sickness and vice: in a word, sin). Love in Jesus' live is revealed as service to others. His ministry is aimed at creating conditions for people to gather together as brothers and sisters who have a common Father.

This way of acting does not enslave the human person, it is not another form of oppression or domination. On the contrary, it creates conditions for the human person to be really free, to take control of his own life, to take on a mission in the world. Christ acts in such a way as to make people free and responsible for their own destiny and that of those around them (Examples: the Samaritan Woman in Jn 4:1-30 and the sinner in Lk 7:36-50).

6. The liberating mission of Christ has a dimension that transcends human values
The love that inspires Jesus, in fulfilling his mission, transcends the human dimension of his personality. No human person is capable of loving with such self-giving. Only someone of divine origin could act in this way.

A person who is not open to the transcendental dimension of life runs the risk of closing in on himself or herself. It is part of human greatness to be able to recognise one's limitations as a creature and the need for divine light to illuminate us in our search for happiness and a correct hierarchy of values. The hope of a more just and fraternal society has its inspiration, ultimately, in a loving God who sustains the universe and reveals himself in human form, through Jesus Christ.

Appendix No. 17B:

Preparation of mini-dramas
(Cut out the following orientations for each group and distribute them)

GROUP 1
Read and reflect on Luke 19:1-10.
• What kind of liberation does Christ show us in this text?
• Present a mini-drama of 4 minutes on the way Christ liberates us today from the slavery of material things.

GROUP 2
Read and reflect on Luke 7:36-50.
• What kind of liberation does Christ show us in this text?
• Present a mini-drama of 4 minutes on the way Christ liberates us from social and class prejudice.

GROUP 3
Read and reflect on Luke 10:25-35.
• What kind of liberation does Christ show us in this text?
• Prepare a mini-drama of 4 minutes on the way Christ frees us from the temptation to despise and reject certain persons in society.

GROUP 4
Read and reflect on Matthew 15: 32-39.
• What kind of liberation does Christ show us in this text?
• Present a mini-drama of 4 minutes on the way Christ frees us from hunger in the world today.

GROUP 5
Read and reflect on John 13: 1-15.
• What kind of liberation does Christ show us in this text?
• Present a mini-drama of 4 minutes on the way Christ frees us oppressive situations.

Appendix No. 18A:

Psychological Profile

a) Objective (Explain beforehand)

This exercise aims at helping the participants to know one another better, so that they can grow as persons, as a group and as a community of faith. This is one of the many types of 'Revision of Life' that can be used to deepen individual conversion and grow as fully human persons. It is important to know the impression we cause on others, especially if this impression is false, so that we can correct our mistakes.

This exercise presupposes qualities of humility and openness towards others and an attitude of faith and courage in facing our own shortcomings. This exercise in fraternal correction is something Jesus proposes after concluding the parable on the lost sheep. He advises: 'If your brother commits a fault, go and take the matter up with him, strictly between yourselves, and if he listens to you, you have won your brother over.'(Mt 18:15).

It is important to avoid, on the one hand, a type of flattery that cloaks over negative points and, as a result, doesn't help the person to grow or, on the other hand, destructive criticism that destroys the other's self-confidence. The spirit that animates the revision of life should be one of faith: 'Where two or three have met together in my name, I am there among them.' (Mt 18:20).

b) Application of the Exercise

Initial orientation

1. The facilitator distributes the appendices (Appendices, 18A, 18B, 18C) and gives a general explanation of the exercise.
2. The participants are divided into small groups of four to six persons. Care should be taken to form groups with people who know one another best. Small groups facilitate greater depth in the Revision of Life and demand less time.
3. Each group elects a co-ordinator. There will be no plenary session. Everything that is said in the group should remain in the group. There should be absolute confidence and trust.

In the groups

4. In the groups, before starting the meeting, the co-ordinator reads the following points:
    a) The exercise starts with a prayer or a Bible reflection. Participants then offer themselves, one by one, to be evaluated by the others. Members are free not to participate. There should be an atmosphere of total liberty.
    b) The evaluation is based on the following questions:
    - What are my positive qualities?
    - What are the shortcomings I need to work at in my life?
5. The person being evaluated can ask questions requesting further information but should not try to defend himself or herself at this stage. He or she can clear up any misunderstandings at the end of the session. He/she should however be aware of the temptation to rationalise and cloak over one's own faults – as the popular saying puts it: 'the truth hurts.' The capacity to acknowledge error is a quality only found in saints and great people.

Growth can be observed when persons are able to make affirmations such as: 'I am beginning to think that I am getting better', 'I am understanding better the point of view of others], 'I now have the reins of my life in my hands', 'I now have open channels of communication with others'…

Without open communication between people, it is difficult to avoid an incomplete and distorted image of others and clear up misunderstandings. It is also difficult to be aware of aspects of one's behaviour and attitudes that can change and should be changed. Open communication creates an environment that favours individual and group growth.

Observation: When the participants of a group are unacquainted, the exercise can be inverted. Instead of each person taking about the person who offers himself/herself to be evaluated, the person can talk about himself/herself, using the same questions:
- What are my positive qualities?
- What are the shortcomings I need to work at in my life?

6. As people evaluate each other, they should avoid two extremes: speaking in a way that offends the other person or, on the other hand, only praising and flattering the person being evaluated. This is a privileged opportunity to diminish the blind area and increase the free area in our lives (See the exercise of Johary's Window, which we presented earlier). This exercise works only in an atmosphere of confidence, mutual respect and faith. The qualities demanded of the participants are: spirit of prayer, respect, humility, confidence, maturity, sincerity and especially charity. To do this exercise without the above conditions can be counterproductive.

This Revision of Life, therefore, demands emotional maturity and acceptance of the other person as he or she is. When we feel we are being respected and valued, our defences fall. We feel free strong enough to take off the masks and put aside the false front we are presenting. It is the price we pay to be able to build community and begin a process of religious conversion. Are we prepared to pay the price?

7. The members of the group should undertake to keep secret what is said in confidence, otherwise people will have a sense of being betrayed.

8. It is advisable to give a few minutes at the beginning of the session so that each person can jot down some ideas on the two question on the sheet supplied (Appendix 18B). The same sheet can be used to note the observations of others.

9. As each person finishes, another person offers himself/herself, voluntarily, to be evaluated. It is important to make it clear that nobody is obliged to accept being evaluated. There should be total freedom.

10. The co-ordinator of the group should control the time so that everyone will have an opportunity to be evaluated. Some tranquillising background music can help the process of reflection.

11. The psychological profile ends with the reading of the parable, "My beloved Bamboo" (Appendix 18C) and with some spontaneous prayer related to people and issues discussed in the group. Each group is free to decide the time of finishing.

Observation: During this exercise the members may want to have a break in the middle of the session. Coffee or tea can be brought to the room where the group is meeting, so that the atmosphere isn't broken by leaving the room.

Appendix No. 18B:

Personal Notes

1. What are my positive qualities?

2. What do I need to improve?

Appendix No. 18C:

My Beloved Bamboo

There was once a marvellous garden, situated in the middle of the countryside. The owner often went on a stroll through the garden, under the midday sun ... For him, a tall, slender bamboo was the most beautiful and esteemed of all the trees and plants in his garden. This bamboo grew and was becoming more and more beautiful. The bamboo knew that his Master loved it and gave him great joy.

One day, the owner, in a pensive mood, approached his beloved bamboo. In a sentiment of profound veneration, the bamboo bent its imposing head. The Master said to the bamboo: 'My dear bamboo, I need you.' The bamboo answered: 'Master, I am ready. Do with me what ever you want.' The bamboo was happy: the great hour of its life seemed to have arrived: the owner was in need and it would serve him. In a grave tone of voice the Master said, 'Bamboo, I could only use you, if I could prune you.'
'Prune? Prune me, Master, please, don't do that. Leave my beautiful figure as it is. You can see how everyone admires me.'
'My beloved bamboo,' the voice of the Master became even more grave, 'it doesn't matter whether people admire you or not. If I can't prune you, I can't use you.'
Silence descended over the garden ... The wind held its breath ... Finally the beautiful bamboo bent over and whispered, 'Master, if you can't use me without pruning me, then ... do with me as you wish.'
'My beloved bamboo, I must also cut your leaves ...'
The sun hid itself behind the clouds ... Some butterflies withdrew frightened ...
The bamboo, trembling and in a low voice, said: 'Master, cut then ...' The Master said again: 'It's still not enough, my beloved bamboo, I need also to *cut you in the middle and take your heart from you*. If I can't do that, I can't use you.'
'Please, Master!', said the bamboo, 'I won't be able to live any more; how can I live without a heart?' 'I must *take out your heart*, otherwise I can't use you.'

A great silence descended over the place ... Some sobbing and suppressed tears ... Then the bamboo bent over until it touched the ground and said: 'Master, prune, cut, split, divide, take it completely, divide out.'

The Master split it. . .
The Master took out its heart.

Afterwards he took it to the middle of the parched land, to a spring where fresh water sprouted out. There the Master carefully put his beloved bamboo on the ground ... He connected one of the ends of the amputated trunks to the spring and the other he placed on the land.

The sprint sang a welcome to the mutilated bamboo. The crystal waters rushed joyfully over the mutilated body of the bamboo, they ran over the parched land, that had pleaded to them so much.

Rice was planted there ... wheat ... maize ... beans ... The days passed ... the seed sprouted ... grew ... everything became green ... the harvest time came ...

In this way, the once marvellous bamboo, in its renunciation, in its annihilation and humility, transformed itself in a *Great Blessing* for all that region.

When it was tall and beautiful, it grew only for itself and was happy with its own beauty. In its renunciation, in its annihilation, in its giving, it became the channel that the Master used to make the lands fertile.

And many men and women have found *life* and have lived from the trunk of a bamboo that has been pruned, cut, split and divided out.

Appendix No. 19A:

4th Theme:
The Church as Community: A Sign of Service to the World

1. Introduction: The Disciples of Christ
Observation: Before starting the talk the speaker can ask the audience for its opinions on the church. How do other people see the church, especially young people?

It is easier to understand the meaning of the church after we have come to know Jesus Christ. The early church was started by people who, on meeting Christ, were attracted by his life style and message. They decided to follow him and continue his mission of love and liberation.

The first community was formed when Christ called each one by name: Andrew, Simon, John, James … and gave them a mission: 'Go and preach the Good News.' The distinguishing mark of this first group of Christians was their faith and confidence in the person of Jesus Christ and their imitation of his way of life and acting. 'The life I now live is not mine, but that which Christ lives in me' (Gal 2:20).

2. Universal Church – The Diocese – The Parish
The parish or small community is the concrete expression of the local church. The church of Jesus Christ exists because there exists, in fact, Christians who live the Christian message in the local parish community. Without the local church, the church of Jesus Christ would be a fiction. Everything that we say about the church, therefore, should be expressed at local level.

Local groups, communities, parishes and pastoral ministries are linked together through a network on diocesan, continental and world levels. The Pope and the bishops are the successors of the apostles. All baptised Christians receive the same invitation of Jesus, 'Go preach to all nations…' Because of its international dimension the church has the ability to overcome barriers caused by national, racial and ethnic differences and unite people as one human family. St Paul reminds us: 'You are all sons of God through faith in Christ Jesus. All baptised in Christ, you have all clothed yourself in Christ, and there are no more distinctions between Jew and Greek, slave and free, male and female, but all of you are one in Christ Jesus.' (Gal 3:28) In a world divided by wars, injustice and animosity, the church has an important moral role in building a better world, in an increasingly globalised society.

3. Models of the Church
While young people today are often open to a spiritual experience, they frequently reject organised religion or the church. So it is important to help them to realise that any important message that needs to be transmitted over time, from one generation to another, can only be done when organisational structures are in place. Without them there is no continuity over time. If we have the gospel today it is because of the church. While structures can kill and distort the spirit of the original message, they are also necessary. So the church needs to be continually renewing itself in order to reflect the original message of Jesus in all its purity.

When young people reject the church, they are often unconsciously rejecting one model of the church. It can be a very freeing experience for them to realise that there is, in fact, another model which is attractive and makes a lot of sense for today's world. And that this is the model we find in the New Testament.

Therefore, an understanding of the different models of church is important in order to comprehend the different expressions of the church around us and also the model which we should be strengthening. Here we will deal with two basic models:
  a) the Clerical Model and
  b) the Community Model.

a) The Clerical Model of Church
Before Vatican II (1965) the clerical or pyramidal model of church was emphasised. This model of church can be represented in the following way:

Here the vision is as follows: God who is all-powerful sent his Son, Jesus Christ, to save us. Jesus Christ shares the same divine nature with the Father and, therefore, is also all-powerful. Jesus nominates one of his disciples, Peter, as a first Pope. The Pope does not have the same power as Jesus, but still has a lot of power. The Pope ordains the bishops. The bishop in his diocese does not have as much power as the Pope, however he has considerable power. The bishop ordains priests. The pastor doesn't have as much power as the bishop. However, in his parish his orders carry considerable weight. In this model the laity don't have any power. Their duty is to obey and carry out the decisions of the clergy.

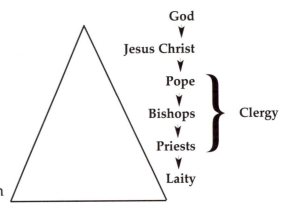

Lay people are mere passive receptors of their orientations. In this model, obedience is a central value. The pastor, for example, is alone responsible for all the decisions taken in his parish. This is a style of leadership has been copied from monarchical societies.

However, this style of leadership is a temptation not only for the clergy. We frequently find a similar authoritarian and centralising leadership among lay leaders.

b) The Community or Ministerial Model of Church
But there is another model. The model we find in the New Testament and which is therefore the model proposed by Jesus Christ. The documents of Vatican II returned to a more biblical model of the use of power in the church. In this model, a circle replaces the pyramid. The fundamental vocation in the church is to be baptised. Through baptism there is a fundamental equality between all Christians; they are all responsible for the church. One of the Pope's titles is 'Servant of the Servants of Christ'.

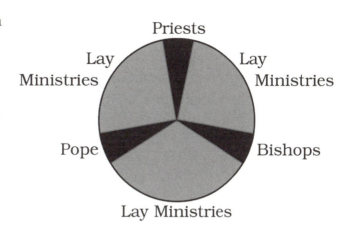

The Latin American bishops, in the Puebla document (1989), spoke of a church of communion and participation. Today we understand the function of the priest as an animator and a bridge that unites the people in a community. The priest is pastor, as Christ was pastor – concerned and willing to give his life for his sheep.

The offices of governing within the church are functions of service, not of domination: 'You know that in the world, rulers lord it over their subjects, and their great men make them feel the weight of authority; but it shall not be so with you. Among you, whoever wants to be great must be your servant and whoever wants to be first must be willing to be the slave of all like the Son of Man. He did not come to be served, but to serve, and to give up his life as a ransom for many' (Mt 20:25-28). St Paul uses the image of the human body. 'Just as a human body, though it is made up of many parts, is a single unit because all these parts, though many, make one body, so it is with Christ. In the one Spirit we were all baptised, Jews as well as Greeks, slaves as well as citizens, and one Spirit was given to us all to drink' (1 Cor 12:12).

In the Acts of the Apostles, the early Christians, we are told, lived in groups and met in small communities. 'The whole group of believers was united, heart and soul ... everything was held in common' (Acts 4:32).

In the community model of church, there are different functions or ministries. These are seen as different ways of serving others: the Pope, the bishops, the priests, the deacons, the religious and the lay ministries. Power in the church is power as service, not power as domination. Jesus Christ is the model.

So we need to put our shoulders to the wheel of change to help accelerate the shift from a clerical to a community model of church.

4. Two Moments of the Church's Existence
The church can be viewed on two levels:
a) the church 'ad intra' and
b) the church 'ad extra'.
These levels correspond to the two central documents of Vatican II. The first document,

Lumen Gentium (Light to the World), describes the church as looking in on itself; while the second document, *Gaudium et Spes* (Joy and Hope), presents the church as going out on mission to the world. The two aspects of the church's life complement each other.

a. The Church looking inward (*Lumen Gentium*)
i) Building community
The document *Lumen Gentium* presents the Church as the People of God, continuing the work of the Good Pastor who has come to serve, not to be served and to give his life for his sheep. The church is the community of persons who believe in the plan of salvation of Jesus.

The concrete union of Christians, however, is not a fact, but rather a task we have to realise. The local church is continually being built. Each Christian, through his or her baptism, is responsible for building the local church so that it will be the mirror of the love of God in the world and sign of his reign.

Each member contributes to the community with his own particular charisma and gifts. The role of the bishop, of the priest and of the lay ministers is one of co-ordinating and maintaining harmony among the charismas.

We need special channels and pastoral structures that favour participation and decision making if the church is to be a true expression of the People of God. These structures can be parish councils, group meetings, assemblies and an evaluation and planning process.

The church is made up of fragile human beings who are sinners. We need to work through conflict. This is part of being human. We are not angels. Therefore, it needs to be continually renewed. At the same time, we are confident in the power of God who guides its steps.

In some dioceses there are different experiments with the formation of smaller communities within parishes so that the community experience is more real.

ii) Liturgical Expression: Eucharist
Christ requested that his Last Supper be renewed. 'Do this in memory of me.' The sacrament of the Eucharist makes Christ's sacrifice present among us, not in the sense of a repetition of his material death, but rather a celebration of his attitude of love and self-giving which led him to make the ultimate gesture of love.

In each Eucharistic celebration Christ repeats to the assembled community: 'This is my body which is given for you.' This self-giving, this alliance of love, which Christ renews each day in the Mass, should lead to an identical attitude on our part, as we attempt to live out the Christian faith in daily life. The Mass presupposes community and is always an act of the community of believers. The Communion is the complete sign of this common-union with our brothers and sisters. We celebrate by anticipation the new world we are working to build.

Mature families feel the need to get together to celebrate what they have in common, share their moments of happiness, exchange ideas and help one another. In this way, as members of God's family, we need to come together to listen to the Word of God, to pray and to deepen our union and charity.

Jesus invites Christians to come together with him around a table to build the Christian community. Celebrating together we learn to live the new life Christ brought into the world.

b. The Church looking out to the world (*Gaudium et Spes*)
The *Gaudium et Spes* document describes the church in relation to the world around her. The church doesn't exist for herself, but rather to serve humanity and build the kingdom of God in today's society. We need to balance the tension of looking inwards upon the community and looking outwards towards the world.

i) The Church and the kingdom
The church doesn't exist as an island, separated from the world. Neither does she exist only to bring the world into her fold. She exists, rather, to serve the world and build the kingdom.

    Leonardo Boff gives a vivid description of the mission of Jesus: 'A surprising thing happens when this young thirty-year-old man realises, before God, that salvation and eternal life depend on him. He starts to tread the dusty roads of Palestine. What does he announce? The church? No. The sacraments? Also no. Himself? No. He announces something which is more important than himself, more fundamental than the church, more radical than the sacraments: he announces the kingdom of God. The first time he appears in public, in the synagogue, he explains that the kingdom of God is neither the church, nor he himself directly, nor simply a part of this world, but constitutes the *oldest dream of the human heart*, the almost desperate aspiration of all human cultures, which resisted all efforts to eradicate it from the human mind: reconciliation, fraternity, the overcoming of everything that alienates human conscience. It announces the filial reconciliation with God. Jesus touches the depth of the human heart. It is where he seeks the kernel of his message, the fundamental reason for hope that impels man to look forward throughout the centuries.'

    The kingdom of God is the biblical expression which signifies the new world that one day will exist because God has promised it: a world of truth, of justice, without misery, without division between rich and poor. A world without abandoned children, without hunger, and no masses of unemployed. A New World which is for the here and now and not only for after death. 'The kingdom of God is in the midst of you' (Lk 17:21). It is the Circle of Life we are called to build.

    The God of Jesus Christ has come to establish his kingdom in a world that is subverting the fundamental values. He has come to put on its feet a world that has since turned up-side-down, to 'free the oppressed' and make 'the poor happy,' 'to bring down from their thrones the powerful and raise up the humble' (Lk 1:46-55; 4:16-22; 6:17-26; 7:18-23).

    The kingdom signifies the gospel plan according to which God is Father and we are sons, daughters, brothers and sisters of one another. St John is very explicit: 'But if any man says, "I love God," while hating his brother, he is a liar. If he does not love the brother whom he has seen, it cannot be that he loves God whom he has not seen. And indeed this command comes to us from Christ himself: "that he who loves God must also love his brother"' (1 Jn 4:20-21).

    Our hope of a better world is based on our belief that this is a fundamental demand of God's plan. For this reason Cardjin could state: "We do not preach revolution. We are the revolution itself.'

    The kingdom, however, cannot be identified with any social or political organisation, no matter how perfect this may be. It goes deeper. It is the Utopian vision, the vision of perfection, which impels men and women to discover and organise more and more perfect historical interventions in preparation for the definitive kingdom, at the end of time.

    The church has received the mission of announcing the kingdom of God and establishing it among the peoples. According to Vatican II, she is the germ and beginning of this kingdom on earth.

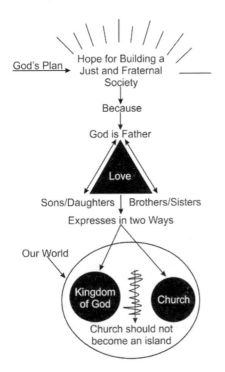

ii) The Church and Non-Christians

We present in the following visual way, the mission of the church in the world:

Those who work for the gospel values (justice, truth, liberty, forgiveness, and the common good) are also working for the kingdom, even though they may not be Christians. These latter, even though lacking an explicit faith, are doing God's will. Those who promote the kingdom are, therefore, not always within the church's fold. On the contrary, historically many of the great promoters of liberty, justice and human rights were outside the church and, at times, were very critical of her lack of prophetic vision and action.

Bishop Oscar Romero wrote a year before he was assassinated by the military dictatorship in El Salvador: 'We are now doing this work of the church of building the kingdom of God. Outside the church also every person who strives for justice, who works for just demands in an unjust environment, is working for the kingdom of God. These people may or may not be Christians. The church does not embrace the whole of the kingdom of God. The kingdom of God extends beyond the frontiers of the church and, therefore, the church appreciates everyone that is tuned in her effort to implant the kingdom of God. A church that works pure, uncontaminated, then, would not be the church of service to men.'

The church is the 'leaven in the mass,' the 'salt' and the 'light} in the world.

The church is the group of people in the world that profess to follow Jesus Christ. Its members have received an explicit revelation of the kingdom from Christ and celebrate his salvific presence through the sacramental signs. The Christian community strives to live a new lifestyle in which the quality of the relationship between its members is based on gospel values. These can preach the kingdom with credibility because they are already striving to live this ideal in community.

Christians, therefore, have a greater responsibility for the building of the kingdom, through the concrete events in history (*LG* 14). While others have to grope in the darkness of night, Christians have the advantage of walking in the light of day. We cannot, therefore, claim ignorance: 'Lord when did we see you hungry and thirsty?' A group of church people that see the church as an island, separated from the rest of the world, turn their backs on Christ's call to be a transforming force in their normal environment of work, study and living.

Appendix No. 19B:

The Kingdom always lies beyond us
Archbishop Oscar Romero, Martyr

We are workers,
It helps now and then to step back and take the long view.
The kingdom is not only beyond our efforts,
It is even beyond our vision.

We accomplish in our lifetime only a tiny fraction
Of the magnificent enterprise that is God's work.
Nothing we do is complete, which is another way of saying,
That the kingdom always lies beyond us.
No statement says all that can be said.
No prayer fully expresses our faith.
No confession brings perfection.
No programme accomplishes the church's mission.
No set of goals and objectives includes everything.

That is what we are about.
We plant the seeds that one day will grow.
We water the seeds that are already planted,
Knowing that they hold future promise.
We lay the foundations that will need further developments.
We provide yeast that produces effects beyond our capabilities.

We cannot do everything,
And there is a sense of liberation in realising that.
This enables us to do something, to do it very well.
It may be incomplete, but it is a beginning, a step along the way,
An opportunity for the Lord's grace to enter and do the rest.
We may never see the end results,
But that is the difference between the master builder and the worker.

We are workers, not master builders,
Ministers, not messiahs.
We are prophets of a future not our own.

Appendix No. 19C:

Questions for discussion on Continuity

Observation: This course can be given to young people on their own, to young people and adults together or to adults on their own. Depending on which group is doing the course one of the following three options of questions for the group debate can be chosen. Or perhaps these questions can inspire other questions that best answer the needs of the participants:

QUESTIONS ON CONTINUITY
(When the course is given to young people on their own)

1. How can we improve our youth group or youth organisation?
If members don't participate in a youth group, what about starting some sort of a youth organisation, at the end of this course?

2. The church exists to build the kingdom of God. To the extent that we promote justice, fraternity, the elimination of prejudice, and promote communion and participation and personal conversion we are helping to make the kingdom present among us. What can we do to make our contribution to the building of a new church and a new society?

3. What can we do to strengthen youth ministry in our parish or diocese?

QUESTIONS ON CONTINUITY
(For courses given to adults on their own)

1. In your opinion, what are the difficulties that prevent us from building the ideal model of church in our parish? Give suggestions to overcome these difficulties?

2. How do you hope to participate in your community or pastoral ministry after this course?

3. How can we reach out and involve young people today?

4. The church exists to build the kingdom of God. To the extent that we promote justice, fraternity, the elimination of prejudice, and promote communion and participation and personal conversion we are helping to make the kingdom present among us. What can we do to make our contribution to the building of a new church and a new society?

QUESTIONS ON CONTINUITY
(For course given on diocesan level)

1. How can we give continuity to this course?

2. What is the best way of organising youth ministry on diocesan level?

3. What contribution can I give to strengthen the diocesan youth organisation?

Appendix No. 20A:

Time Management – Self Evaluation

Instructions: After each question place a mark in column true or false (in a general way)

Observation: This is not an exam where you should try to get better notes that the others. It is rather a tool to help you to discover the skills that you are lacking and which you can acquire.

	TRUE	FALSE
01. I have difficulties in meeting deadlines and/or commitments.	( )	( )
02. With reasonable frequency I find myself explaining again instructions or information.	( )	( )
03. When faced with two tasks that are equally important, I always pick the most pleasant to be done first.	( )	( )
04. I become involved in tasks that others could or should do.	( )	( )
05. A day that has no novelties or emergencies is tiring.	( )	( )
06. I lose interest in projects, works or negotiations that last too long or delay in arriving at a conclusion.	( )	( )
07. I sometimes try to share a decision or ask the opinion of yet another person, even though I have the information to act on.	( )	( )
08. I become involved in tasks that have already been finished so as to improve them.	( )	( )
09. I rarely have time to plan the activities of the following day	( )	( )
10. I frequently interrupt tasks to deal with something urgent that has suddenly appeared.	( )	( )
11. I prefer not to take a decision if it involves running many risks.	( )	( )
12. Much of my time is spent correcting the work of others.	( )	( )
13. I continually find myself having to do many tasks with little time – without any planning or preparation	( )	( )
14. My subordinates and/or colleagues don't always understand the instructions I give.	( )	( )
15. I have a tendency to postpone tasks that are not urgent.	( )	( )
16. I sometimes feel lost in my area of work.	( )	( )
17. I frequently correct my own work because of mistakes made in the execution of previous tasks.	( )	( )
18. At times I find myself dispersed or thinking of other things.	( )	( )
19. I solve problems independent of knowing or not the causes.	( )	( )
20. I have difficulty in putting into practice the solutions to problems even when the solution is clear.	( )	( )
21. I think it is a waste of time trying to foresee future problems.	( )	( )
22. I like to continue thinking about what I am going to do after work or on weekends.	( )	( )
23. I try to solve problems as they arise.	( )	( )
24. If I give a task to someone it will mean a lot of explanations, so I prefer to do it myself.	( )	( )

Instructions for synthesis of answers

In the following columns, place a circle around the numbers that appear in the column marked 'TRUE' (you can ignore the numbers that are marked in the column marked 'FALSE') and afterwards verify how many numbers you marked and then calculate the totals. For example, if you make a circle around the numbers 5, 13 and 17 in column I, the total below will be 3.

COLUMN I	COLUMN II	COLUMN III	COLUMN IV
1	2	3	4
5	6	7	8
9	10	11	12
13	14	15	16
17	18	19	20
21	22	23	24
—	—	—	—

Totals of numbers circled:

Identification of the individual style of Time Management

Transfer the totals of each column I, II, III, IV to the tables below:

Totals	Style of Time Management		
COLUMN I	Fast decisions (Fire-fighter)	____	( )
COLUMN II	No Focus (Scattered)	____	( )
COLUMN III	Indecisive (Mañana)	____	( )
COLUMN IV	Do it yourself (Perfectionist)	____	( )

Style 1: Firefighter (Rapid and unreflected decisions)
A fast-decision person works from a day to day basis. Normally he has no work plan. For this reason, he/she spends the most of the time 'putting out fires' instead of anticipating and avoiding the development of future problems. The person justifies his way of working by saying that crises are inevitable.

Due to the 'emergency' nature of his/her day this type of person works under a lot of pressure and is always faced with the need to take on the spot decisions, often without the necessary information. He prefers to work in this way, since he feels he is always occupied and contributing.

The questions that reveal symtoms of wasting time:
  01 & 09 ...... A. Inadequate Planning
  05 & 21 ...... B. Crisis Management
  13 & 17 ...... C. Hurry. Actions without the necessary information

Style 2: Lack of focus (Scattered)
The person without focus tries to do many things at the same time and ends up not doing any of them well. His/her focus of attention changes rapidly from one task to another. Consequently, it is rare when something which has been started is finished. There is a lack of self-discipline to remain working on the accomplishment of a set task for a long period of time. His/her table, or folder is always cluttered with things to be done.
The information that he transmits to the members of the organisation is not clear. He feels he lacks time to give explanations. Information is rarely at hand.

The questions that reveal symtoms of wasting time:
  02 & 14 . . . . . . D. Inefficient communication
  06 & 10 . . . . . . E. Unfinished tasks
  22 & 18 . . . . . . .F. Lack of concentration

Style 3: Indecisive (Mañana)
An indecisive person doesn't like the responsibility of taking decisions. When possible he throws the responsibility onto the shoulders of others or postpones these decisions as far as possible, because he feels insecure in accomplishing them.
 This person, normally, believes that he works better under pressure. He has difficulties in understanding the causes of problems and tries to treat only the symptoms.

The questions that reveal symtoms of wasting time:
  11 & 07 .... G. Indecisive – fear of failing.
  03 & 15 .... H. Procrastination – postponing the accomplishing of tasks.
  19 & 23 .... I. Difficulties in making a diagnosis of problem.

Style 4: Perfectionist (Leave it to me)
Obviously it is important to do things well. The perfectionist, however, goes further. She does not trust others. She centralises. She believes that they won't do things as well as she does them, and therefore is reluctant to delegate. This is the type of person who likes to do everything herself. She is a perfectionist and likes to verify if each detail is correct. She does not tolerate the errors of others and considers them incompetent. Therefore, she spends much time 'doing' rather than 'managing'.

The questions that reveal symtoms of wasting time:
  04 & 24 ...... J. Lack of delegation.
  16 & 20 ...... K. Inadequate control.
  08 & 12 ...... L Perfectionism

Observation: The objective of this exercise is to discover our faults so that we can correct them. Therefore, we shouldn't feel depressed if the general result is negative. The results may be a little exaggerated. The aim is to awaken us to the need to address this problem in our lives.

Summary of the Symtoms of Wasting Time

a. Inadequate Planning:
- Difficulty in foreseeing or anticipating future problems.
- Difficulty in developing plans for solving problems
- Difficulty in establishing deadlines.
- Difficulty in giving importance to the need of a process of working towards objectives.

b. Crisis Administration
- Difficulty in establishing a procedure for solving problems.
- Too much time spent in 'putting out fires' rather than preventing them.
- Making last minute decisions rather than being concerned with analysing problems in advance.
- Difficulty in avoiding constant interruptions.
- Being constantly in a state of panic.

c. Hurry: Actions undertaken without the necessary information
- Sudden decision making.
- Attempts to carry out an excessively large volume of work within the constraints of an excessively short deadline.
- Hurry to finish a task. Impatience with details.
- Difficulty in establishing priorities.
- Difficulty in collecting and analysing relevant information.
- Taking hurried decisions without first acquiring and analysing the relevant information.

d. Inefficient communication
- Using inadequate channels for transmitting instructions and information.
- Lack of clarity in communication.
- Lack of feedback.
- Lack of attentive listening.
- Difficulties in interpreting the objectives and plans with reference to the activities of your area of work.

e. Unfinished tasks
- Lack of follow-up of objectives, priorities and deadlines.
- Lack of self-discipline for completing tasks.
- Continually changing tasks (or objective) through lack of interest.
- Difficulty in taking on responsibilities.

f. Lack of concentration
- Lack of self-discipline for working with longer deadlines.
- Tendency to daydream by wandering off to other topics.
- Easily distracted.
- When necessary he/she is not able to plan the necessary isolation.

g. Indecision: fear of failure
- Lack of confidence in your skill for making decisions.
- Attempts to pass on responsibilities to others.

- Lack of the ability to run risks when making decisions, due to fear of failure.
- Rarely makes things happen. He/she waits for things to happen.
- Difficulty in evaluating alternatives in terms of time, risk and viability.

h. *Procrastinating: Putting off the accomplishment of tasks*
- Tendency to put off the execution of a task when there is time for doing it.
- Excessive time spent in working with tasks we like rather than with priority tasks.
- Frequent interruptions that you yourself introduce, e.g. frequent coffee breaks, courtesy visits, etc.
- Difficulty in establishing priorities.

i. *Difficulty in making a diagnosis of problems*
- Inability to distinguish between causes and symptoms.
- Not search for necessary information.
- Lack of adequate analyse of problems.
- Difficulty in identifying driving and restrictive forces.
- Difficulty in identifying opportunities.

j. *Lack of delegation*
- Doing the work that subordinates (or others) could or should do.
- Excessive time spent with routine work and details.
- Giving responsibility without the necessary authority.
- Difficulty in training collaborators.

k. *Inadequate control*
- Lack of records or control in your work or that of the organisation.
- Difficulties in establishing intermediary or final deadlines.
- Confuses records with control.

l. *Perfectionist*
- Excessive time spent in finishing everything with perfection.
- Excessive time spent in correcting the work of others.
- Not finishing any work, always thinking of the possibility of improving it.
- Difficulty in establishing standards of achievement for oneself and for others.

Group Work

Read the different styles of time management and discuss the following questions:
1. What are your greatest difficulties for managing your time?
2. What are the consequences of the style of time management you have adopted?
3. How could you begin to solve some of your difficulties?

Appendix No. 20B:

5th Theme:
Techniques of Time Management
(Suggestions for avoiding burnout, emotional imbalance and superficiality)

Initial Observations: The Problems We Face

1. Last minute Improvising:
The lack of planning, the lack of organisation and foresight can do serious damaged to the quality of everything we do.

We need to plan and follow through. How often, at the end of a day, of a week, or of a month, we are left with the impression of having done nothing, of having drifted. We wasted time because we did not know how to organise ourselves.

When the virus of disorganisation infects, damage is done to the different commitments we undertake. Frustration and discouragement increase as plans fail to materialise. A youth leader put it well: 'The child of improvisation is superficiality.' Instead of growth we have stagnation and superficiality. The best and more dynamic people leave an organisation. A dynamic person about to abandon a chaotic church movement remarked to me: 'Serious people don't waste time.'

2. Burnout: The damage done is not only to an organisation or pastoral ministry but also to those who are in positions of responsibility.

Today, we know that many diseases such as burnout, ulcers, and heart problems have psychosomatic causes. And the principal cause is anxiety. In the past, these were sickness of older people. Today, the pressures, tasks and tensions of modern living have added many young people to the list of patients.

People in positions of responsibility are part of this high-risk group. A young person, for example, who studies, works, dedicates time to leisure activities and youth ministry, must be an organised person if she is to avoid burnout.

3. Anxiety: Prolonged anxiety is a sign that burnout is just around the corner. It is the red light pointing to the lack of oil in the engine. Anxiety alerts us to a possible threat that demands immediate action. Many of us, for example have had a similar experience when we escaped from a serious accident. Our entire body entered into a state of alert to find an immediate solution to the imminent threat of serious injury.

Anxiety as a defence mechanism is necessary for facing emergencies. But prolonged anxiety cannot be the normal state of a person. When such is the case, reserve energy is drained away and the body is worn down. Lost energy can only be recovered by returning to a state of relaxation.

When anxiety leads to burnout, there is a dramatic change in people's lives. They lose initiative, enthusiasm and joy of living. Bad health obstructs their work. The quality of work suffers. There is no motivation to do anything. They are easily irritated by others. They have no patience. Conflicts flare up over trivia. The line is overloaded and any additional charge blows the fuse. Their lack of control provokes a sense of fright and panic.

Few leaders reach this extreme. Many, however, are moving in that direction.

4. ***Burnout is not caused by too much work***: Many people believe that burnout is caused by too much work. This is often not so. A successful leader can have a lot of work and at the same time lead a perfectly balanced life. Two rules, however, must be followed:
   i) The person must have a positive attitude to her many commitments, seeing them as a challenge, opportunity to develop talents, to create something new, and to help others. A public person once coined the phrase: 'Our duty should become our pleasure.'
   ii) Leaders must have the organisational skills for dealing with many tasks at the same time.

   In the following lines we will discuss suggestions for avoiding burnout, emotional imbalance and superficiality in our pastoral work, and in our lives (since pressures can come from a variety of sources). These are suggestions that will help us to hold on to our dynamism, enthusiasm, and enjoyment of life – in the midst of many commitments. At the same time, we should not confuse spontaneity with improvisation and lack of organisation. Organisation is power. Power can be used to build a better world or preserve an unjust one. If we are serious about changing the world with the message of the gospel, we cannot ignore the importance of organisation and the power that goes with it. When we are organised, things get done; when we are not, we remain on the frustrating level of empty promises.

5. *Clear goals:* Organisation presupposes goals. People organise themselves in order to attain goals. And goals involve a clear theory or philosophy of youth ministry. Clear goals stimulate action and motivate us to make sacrifices in order to move forward. When we are not clear where we are going, our enthusiasm and motivation rapidly evaporate.

   Having made these initial observations we can now examine some techniques that facilitate personal organisation and efficiency.

Plan Your Time

1. Create habits:
(a) Use of time
How we use our time, therefore, is important. The quality of leaders is measured, not by the quantity of time available, but by the use they make of the available time. The best leaders, in general, have little free time; the worst leaders often have a lot of time. There are only 24 hours in the day and leaders have a limited amount of time available to deal with commitment. Many people today have a multiplicity of activities tugging at their available time: study, work, and sports, peer group activities, family commitments, church activities, dating … There is only one solution: time management.

Planning requires time. Yet when we plan we gain time and get better results. People who have developed the ability to plan their time are more efficient and eliminate many sources of anxiety and burnout in their lives.

b. Habits automate the process:
Now for an important alert! To plan your time it is not enough to listen to a talk on the topic or to read a book. Knowing the theory does not mean you can automatically put it into practice. We need to create habits. In one of my courses a participant put it this way: 'We need to create habits. I have already acquired many of these habits of organisation and others I need to work at so they can become part of my daily routine.'

We need to practice the following suggestions until they become habits – in the same way as we learn to walk, to talk, to write, to type, to play a guitar, to ride a bicycle, to drive a car, or to play football. When we form habits, the subconscious mind executes certain tasks automatically, without the need for our conscience mind to be concerned with them. This automation frees our mind to dedicate ourselves to more important tasks. And positive habits eliminate unnecessary anxiety and tensions.

Positive habits are not acquired from one day to another. Training is necessary; so are self criticism and self discipline. It is an illusion to think of forming habits without paying the price: the price of self discipline. We have no right to co-ordinate others if we do not know how to co-ordinate ourselves. We cannot be at the helm of other people's lives if we are not at the helm of our own.

2. Take notes

a. Basic rule: write it down

Don't trust your memory; write it down. The mere act of writing down helps to clarify our ideas. There is consensus among experts about the basic rule of planning: the need to write down commitments, ideas and inspirations, immediately they come to mind. If you need to discuss five different items with a youth leader – the next time we meet – you must write them down.

This is a simple rule. You take note of commitments to guarantee their execution. You take note of ideas and inspirations to present them in future meetings, to use them to prepare talks or articles, to develop a clearer vision of youth ministry. Notes should be made at the moment of inspiration, as ideas can vanish in a flash. The solution for a problem in the youth ministry was not registered? Months later the idea was remembered, but it was now too late.

b. Use an appointment book or diary:

Commitments noted on loose pieces of paper end up being lost. The absence of an appointment book can mean commitments are forgotten or scheduled for the same time. It can also mean that time is not reserved for preparing meetings, talks, encounters, trips. An appointment book is an essential tool. A larger desk appointment book can be used, but a pocket appointment book has the advantage of being easily carried about and taken out at any moment to check commitments and schedule others.

c. Where do we write new ideas or reminders? A Master List.

An appointment book on its own is not sufficient. We need to jot down different commitments and ideas as they present themselves: suggestions, inspirations, telephones calls, things to be done and contacts to be made on a master list. Some people make the mistake of writing different lists on different pieces of paper and leaving them in different places. This is a sure formula for confusion and inefficiency. If you are in a situation where you have no other option, make sure to transfer the ideas immediately to the master list, at the first available opportunity.

Other lists. Major tasks on your master list should be broken down into smaller components. The preparation of a course, for example, can be broken down into: scheduling of meeting, preparation of inscription forms, contact with speakers, reservation of retreat centre, preparation of talk … The master list is a container from which appointments and commitments can be written into a daily list and other lists.

Items from the master list can be transferred daily to other lists. As each item is transferred, it is deleted from the master list. People use different systems. Some people use the blank pages in an appointment book for the different lists. Other people prefer to use a spiral notebook instead or a card system. Each person should have a system that best suits her personality type. I personally use a card system for the following lists: master list, daily list, future commitments, telephones calls, inspirations and ideas, suggestions for meetings, issues to be discussed with others, etc. Items from the master list are transferred each day to a daily list, a phone list, and a future list. Items that have no urgency go on to a future list. Sometimes smaller tasks can be grouped together. For example, you may wish to make all the telephone calls at the same time.

Cards of different colours can be used to distinguish the different lists and can be kept within the pages of a pocket appointment book. Colours make it easy to locate and recall rapidly important information for decisions making. Having the cards with the pocket appointment book means they are readily available.

It is not enough, however, to take notes. In a meeting Paul confessed: 'I write down commitments, but afterwards I forget to consult my appointment book.' So Paul needs to create the habit of consulting his appointment book. He needs to practice this skill as he would any other one.

3. Have Priorities

a. Distinguish priorities from secondary issues: Once a list of commitments has been made, a second step is necessary: We need to distinguish between:

what is has priority from what is secondary;
what is urgent and cannot be postponed
what depends on others (and therefore the other should be dealt with first),
what can be left for afterwards.

This step, therefore, involves the organisation of commitments in a hierarchical order of importance. Thus we can give more time and attention to more important commitments and avoid wasting time with lesser ones. We need to keep our eye on the ball and avoid being side-tracked by superficial and secondary issues. We need to focus. If we spread our out lines too much, we can't advance and we may be defeated. If we give the same importance to everything, we do nothing in depth. Everything is done superficially. Here we have one of the causes of stagnation and superficiality in youth ministry.

Competent leaders give priority to certain commitments in their pastoral work. Knowing where to concentrate time and energy is one of the characteristics of dynamic leadership.

When there are no priorities, that which is urgent becomes a priority. That which is urgent is, in general, is a consequence of lack of planning, improvisation, incapacity to foresee situations needing attention, and lack of preparation. A leader who has no priorities can be compared to a goalkeeper in a training session who faces different players shooting for goal at the same time. If he attempts to catch all the balls he ends up catching none.

On the other hand, planning has to be flexible. Provision has to be made for the unexpected and the unforeseen. 'I reserved an evening to prepare a text. A friend unexpectedly came in to discuss a problem. I had to change my plan,' explained a church leader. The non acceptance of the unforeseen can increase anxiety and the possibility of burnout. Church ministry is based on deep human relations. An efficient organisation must somehow integrate this aspect of ministry.

b. Make a daily list:
So start each day by making a list of your commitments, organising them in order of importance. 'The day is the smallest unit and is the easiest to be administered in the systematic programming of our time. If you have no control over your daily routine of work, it will be impossible to have plans for longer periods, such as a month or a year.' Here we are talking not only of pastoral commitments. We need to manage as a whole the commitments of youth ministry, of school, of professional work, of family, of leisure …

Making out a list in the morning takes only a few minutes. The list should be made before getting into the daily bustle. Some isolation is necessary, even if it is only for a few minutes, at home, on the bus … As we make the list, we can erase what has already been done and include unfinished business of the previous day in our new list.

c. Do one thing at a time:
Start by doing one thing at a time. Pass to another item only after finishing the previous one. This increases concentration and quality of work. Be careful not to leave more boring and difficult items for the last – a phenomenon knows as 'replacement activities'. We keep putting off the more difficult tasks and replacing them with enjoyable ones, with the result that the difficult tasks – often the more important ones – never get done.

Start tomorrow making out your list, and continue until the habit automatises this process in your life. At the beginning, be demanding on yourself. Do not allow exceptions. You will be surprised with the change. A new experience of peace, serenity and confidence grows. You are in control of what is taking place around you. You are no longer being tossed about helplessly by events. The writing down of commitments and ideas leads to a free and tranquil mind. Anxiety is substituted by a normal and healthy concern that facilitates concentration on the work to be done. The level of motivation and satisfaction increases to the extent that different commitments are accomplished. A pastoral ministry gains credibility by the seriousness of its work. Criticism diminishes and praise increases. An organised person stands out as a leader and relates to others in a calm and confident manner. He is not flustered and in a state of panic because of urgent matters which he has not prepared for or foreseen.

4. Delegate

Once a list of commitments is made out in order of importance, the next step is to verify the tasks that can be done by others. Centralisation is the death knell of most leaders. Many leaders are overburdened because they don't know how to delegate. An effective leader is not one who does the work of ten, but rather one who encourages ten to work. Delegating responsibilities is an important way of economising time. Delegation means using the knowledge and experience of others. Efficiency increases; new leadership is formed.

Delegating is an art:
i) Tasks should be delegated taking into account people's gifts and talents. One should not contract as a life guard a person who does not know how to swim!
ii) The art of delegating involves making clear what has to be done and a deadline for completing the task. Written instructions avoid misunderstanding.
iii) Follow-up: Some co-ordinators commit the error of delegating without following up. A competent leader accompanies the work being done while avoiding unnecessary interference. He is careful to show confidence in people. As the deadline draws nearer some system of accountability should be set in motion.

5. Identify the 'thieves of time'
A further step is to study work habits in order to identify the time-wasters that daily consume your precious time. Often at the end of a day you have the sensation of having accomplished very little. It is a sign that the thieves of time have taken charge.

After some weeks, you can identify where you are wasting time: continuous interruptions, time spent on unimportant tasks, delay in starting, too much time dedicated to agreeable tasks, lack of delegation, of self-discipline, of method. One of the biggest time wasters can be meetings that are rambling discussions, without any agenda, without any time for beginning or ending, without method, without proper co-ordination, and without concrete conclusions. Once the time-wasters have been identified, you must then take steps to eliminate them.

6. Use a Filing System
What you do with the papers that come in is one of the secrets of keeping on top of things. People in a leadership position need a system for filing documents, texts, letters, articles, books, cutting from newspapers. Leaders often need to prepare talks, articles, texts and proposals for courses, discussion groups, and local newspapers. It is difficult to do a good job without adequate resource material. We gain time and are more effective when we can find necessary information rapidly.

Organisation should not be confused with being neat. People have different visual temperaments. Some people prefer to work with a clear desk, while others prefer a cluttered desk. Both can be organised. The test is whether they can find things easily.

When papers come in you have four options: i) throw them into a *waste paper basket*, ii) put them into a *folder marked action*, iii) put them into a *folder marked holding*, or iv) *file them*. Instead of folders you may use shelves. Processing the action papers (letters to be written, answers to be given, appointments to be set up, meetings to be scheduled, etc.) is at the heart of a good management system. Some papers will go from an action folder to a holding folder. These are the papers that you are holding until a final decision. A letter you send, for example, to someone, inviting her to give a talk at a youth seminar would go into this holding folder. A useful follow up system is to write a reminder in your appointment calendar on a date that you would expect to have heard from her. If she has not replied by that date you can follow up with a phone call or invite someone else.

Finally, some papers need to be filed so that you can find them when necessary. Here there is often a fear of putting important papers into a filing system and not being able to find them again. This is the problem of a badly defined filing system. Each folder should be labelled with a broad general name that can be easily remembered: correspondence, courses, prepared talks, co-ordination committee meetings, miscellaneous, addresses, finances. Articles and texts can be put under such headings as: spirituality, church, adolescent psychology, social problems, youth culture. General headings can be subdivided if necessary: correspondence-received, correspondence-answered. An effective pastoral ministry depends on the capacity of the youth leader to locate timely information for dealing with different situations. This can only be done with an effective filing system.

7. The importance of preparation
a. Preparation is the secret formula for success. Jesus relates the parable of the five prudent and five foolish virgins (Mt 25:1-13). The five foolish virgins were refused entrance to the wedding feast because they had gone after oil for their lamps when the bridegroom arrived. They were not prepared. Their attitude was: let's-leave-it-for-the-last-minute-

and-then-we'll-work-something-out. At the last minute it is often too late. The secret of a good talk, meeting, course, or assembly is in the preparation.

Preparation presupposes a capacity to look ahead and foresee necessary steps to be taken rather than leaving things for the last minute. The capacity to look ahead presupposes writing down commitments and putting them in a hierarchical order of importance. But there is also a further step. Leaders need to look ahead to figure out when they can prepare different commitments before they come on top of them.

The youth leader is like a football player. He is always thinking ahead. A good player is always 'reading' the game and anticipating where the ball is going to fall. He tries to be there beforehand, and in the best position to shoot for goal.

b. Don't Procrastinate: One of the enemies of preparation is procrastination: leaving for tomorrow what can be done today. Angela had to update a document, voted on in an evaluation and planning assembly of youth delegates. The document had to be discussed and approved for publication in the next meeting of the co-ordination committee. The task would take half an hour. During the month before the meeting she kept putting off the task. On the day of the meeting she had nothing to present.

A person who postpones for tomorrow what can be done today, begins a never-ending process of delay and accumulation of work. As the amount of work to be done increases, the anguish and inefficiency grows.

Sometimes there is no urgency in preparing a task. Then a new danger may arise: that of forgetting. A diocesan co-ordination committee decided to prepare internal statutes for the diocesan assembly of the following year. Paul was asked to prepare a draft to be discussed in the following meeting. He was also asked to send a copy to the members before the meeting so they could come prepared. Paul did not take note of his task. Since a number of months would elapse before the next meeting he decided to put off the preparation. He ended up forgetting. Much time was lost in the meeting trying to draw up a text. Due to the limitations of time and the lack of necessary resource material the task was not accomplished.

Some sort of strategy-for-not-forgetting needs to be worked out when the deadline for completing the task is distant. Some people, for example, make a note in their appointment calendar along side the date of the scheduled meeting. Suggestions and ideas that arise before the event are also noted in the same place.

People procrastinate, sometimes, because they are afraid to face into a task that appears to be too large and overwhelming. The task needs to be broken down into smaller units and attacked one at a time.

c. Take advantage of the small units of time: It is not necessary to prepare tasks at once, as a block. Let us suppose you were entrusted with the task of preparing study material for a meeting or for school. There are different stages that can be worked on beforehand: finding relevant material, reading the material, asking for suggestions from colleagues, and making out the first draft. Part of this work can be done during 'smaller units of time' wedged in between different commitments during the day: during lunch hour, travelling by bus, waiting in line. Working on certain stages beforehand has the advantage of getting your subconscious mind moving. The subconscious is a 'genius' and has capacities that in some ways outstrip the conscious mind. The subconscious will work on the existing data twenty-four hours a day – even when you are sleeping. It will present new suggestions to your conscious mind. It is sufficient to start concentrating on the theme and the subconscious begins the work of research. The advantage of working with 'small units of time' over the system of a large block of time is that the subconscious has more time to analyse information and come up with new ideas.

d. Avoid Interruptions: Some tasks demand isolation. If I am preparing a long text and am being continually interrupted by telephones and people wanting to talk to me, it becomes difficult to concentrate. Each time I return to the text my mind delays in focusing again. It becomes difficult to maintain concentration, to remember the overall plan, coherency, and unity between ideas.

Isolation is necessary for certain tasks that demand more concentration and a longer block of time. In homes where this type of isolation is difficult, a solution is to programme a time during the day in which interruptions are avoided. This time is programmed in the same way as one reserves time for a visit, a meeting, and a contact with someone. People get to know that there is a 'sacred time' when you should not be disturbed. You can also get up earlier or stay later after work when everyone else has gone home. It may be necessary to work for some time outside the premises: in the house of a friend, in the local library, in a retreat house, in a room in the parish, in a school.

e. Keep your motivation strong: The preparation of weightier tasks can demand strong motivation to guarantee perseverance. The flames of motivation have to be kept burning, by convincing yourself continually of the importance of the work you are undertaking, and especially, by establishing immediate goals with clear deadlines. It does not matter if the deadlines have to be revised. Deadlines are important to maintain a healthy pressure. Without this pressure (created consciously by yourself) the tendency is to never finish. A young person at university has this problem. There are so many things to be studied and prepared during the year that she needs to establish goals and deadlines: 'I will read this book during the coming week; I will begin to write a paper tomorrow; next week I will start revising the course material for a final exam.'

When writing one of my more recent books I myself had to use these principles of motivation. As a first phase I gathered material, read books (over a hundred of them), revised my notes (jotted down over a seven-year period), and put the relevant ideas on a computer. I did this during two years, in the midst of other commitments. Each day, and each week, I had to decide what books, what material. I had to establish deadlines for myself. The deadlines kept the pressure on so that I could remain committed to my goal. The satisfaction of attaining immediate goals increased the motivation. After two years, I began writing. I spent a few days each week in a retreat house to avoid constant interruptions and distractions. In this second phase, I had to decide what chapters to write first and organise the ideas in subtitles and paragraphs. I started with the easiest and least complicated chapter – not the first – as I needed to see something concrete emerge after such a long effort. Then I worked at each unit at a time, establishing as a goal several units for each day.

At different times, during the two and a half years, I was tempted to quit. I had gathered an enormous quantity of material. It was a lot of work. It seemed there was no end. I needed to work on my motivation. Motivation is like the gasoline in an engine; without it nothing takes place. The division in smaller units, the setting of short term, medium and long-term goals, the pressure of time and the realisation of the importance and influence of the work, were fundamental in keeping motivation at a high level.

Setting Deadlines: Deadlines have to be set. Without the pressure of deadlines we are at the mercy of Parkinson's law: 'The work increases to meet the time available.' If we have a week to do some work, we will take a week. If we have a year to do the same work, we will take a year. Here we meet one of the impasses in youth ministry. Some youth leaders undertake important and crucial tasks at meetings – they start but don't finish. Their past life is filled with abandoned projects.

f. Speed Reading: Speed reading of texts, documents and books is an important way of economising on time and increasing efficiency. It is important to practice this skill using some of the following suggestions:

- i) Do not move your head from one side to another as you read each line.
- ii) Do not move your lips or pronounce the words.
- iii) Do not go back on what you have already read.
- iv) Each time you change focus, increase the span of your reading, making an effort to include groups of words rather than isolated ones,
- v) Start with the second or third word of each line in order not to waste peripheral vision on the margins.

g. Follow your body's rhythm: It is important to consider the rhythm of your body. As we go through the day there is a rise and fall in metabolism of our bodies. There is a rise and fall of energy. Our hormones change. There are times when we are at our best and times when we are less productive. We say some people are morning persons and others are night persons. 'The maximum level of performance normally occurs during the morning. During the rest of the day it is difficult to reach the same level. In the afternoon, the well know after-lunch-period of inactivity starts. Some people try to remain active by using large doses of coffee. This, however, does not solve the problem. Then, in the middle of the evening, after a second phase of high accomplishment, the performance curve begins to decline. It reaches its lowest level a few hours before midnight.'

This rhythm functions for most people. Nevertheless, there are some who work best at night or in the evening. Each youth leader should discover her own periods of most active performance. This rhythm can also change at different periods in your life. You can change, for example, from being a morning person to being an evening person.

It may be convenient to programme work that demands most concentration and clear thinking for the periods of highest performance. Moments of lowest performance can be reserved for personal contacts or lighter work.

8. Systematic Follow-up:

Systematic follow-up is the only way to guarantee continuity.

a. Maintain a vision of the whole (helicopter vision): The leader who works with co-ordination teams must have a global vision of the organisation or pastoral ministry and not just of one particular aspect. He cannot be concerned only with the task of the moment. The leader must be able to see the forest and not just the trees. One university student described her adult director as 'one more member' of her youth group. He lacked the wider vision, the knowledge that should be expected of an adult youth minister.

A person with a global vision of youth ministry as a whole can make a correct evaluation of the situation; he knows the sectors that are doing well and those that need special attention; he perceives the sectors that are taking off. A global vision of the whole, of all sectors, is the first step toward a systematic follow-up of any church or social work.

b. Leadership skills: An important 'time-waster' is the lack of leadership skills. The leader who does not know how to evaluate, plan, perceive solutions for impasses, propose solutions and draws conclusions, wastes a lot of time (his own and others). Sometimes, for example, it is necessary to schedule three meeting when one should be sufficient to deal with a particular topic. The unnecessary multiplication of meetings is caused by lack of leadership skills for co-ordinating meetings, controlling time, and drawing conclusions.

The use of a notebook is important to economise on time and guarantee continuity. Writing all your notes in one notebook makes it easy to find things.

During meetings, discussions set off new ideas in people's minds. Sometimes these ideas are unconnected with the immediate point being discussed. Often it is not possible or pedagogical to present them at that particular moment. To do so would break the sequence of the discussion. However, group members need to have a system of jotting reminders at the side of a page where they can easily remember to bring them up at the appropriate moment. This is also a way of taking the pressure off people who feel impelled to continually throw in 'red herrings' into the discussion.

c. Communication: We live in a technological age and we need to use the tools available to socialise information. Different means of communication can economise on time. Many of our projects fail through lack of communication, bad communication or delayed communication.

Letters: Communication by letter has the advantage of eliminating ambiguity and misunderstanding, common to oral communication. Through letters we avoid unnecessary journeys, we reach more people and we keep youth informed and motivated.

Telephone, Fax, E-mail: Most leaders have access to telephones and the Internet (at home, in their workplace, on the street, in the parish). For some tasks a fax or e-mail can economise on time. In a short time we can consult others, pass on information, and schedule a meeting. Some people make a visit or a journey when a telephone or an e-mail would be the most appropriate and efficient means of communication. However, we need to learn skills of telephone communication. Using a telephone is different from a face-to-face conversation. We need to organise our ideas beforehand to diminish costs and be more efficient.

Events already scheduled: Much time can be saved if we take advantage of events already scheduled. In an encounter, for example, I will be meeting certain people. I need to pass on a text to one, discuss a problem with another, invite a young person to participate in a course, schedule a meeting. In the encounter it is possible to make these contacts, in a short time – that is, if I have organised my list.

9. Know when to say 'No'

There are times when we should say no. Leaders who take on too many commitments may end up doing nothing in depth and even harming their health.

Youth leaders are usually capable and generous people. They like what they do. They are responsible and capable people and so receive numerous requests to become involved in many things. Invitations are sometimes attractive and it can be difficult to refuse. The leader has to discern what to accept and what to refuse.

10. Have patience with the limitations of others: The model of an organised leader we are presenting here is different from the efficient and cold business executive who treats others as so many cogs in an engine. Leaders demand efficiency – but in a nice way. They need to be tolerant. 'Without intelligent tolerance of errors . . . it is difficult to motivate people. In church ministry and other types of volunteer work, we have to win the confidence of people. Human warmth is important. Organisational structures should promote a community spirit, fundamental for the living out of the gospel message.

11. Maintain a balance: We need to balance efficiency with affection. Some personality types have a strong tendency to overemphasise efficiency and underestimate the importance of informal chats and friendships. Other personality types tend to swing to the opposite extreme. We need to maintain a middle course between efficiency and affection. Young people are often in situations in which the emotional elements are decisive.

12. Know how to recreate yourself: The generosity and idealism of some people can lead them to such dedication that they forget their own need for relaxation. People are not machines. They need moments of rest to recuperate their lost energies and avoid burnout.

Some relax by chatting, others by sleeping, having a beer together, playing sports, going to the movies, going on outings, listening to music. Others do relaxation and breathing exercises. Discover what works best for you and make it part of your planning.

13. Develop a spirituality that gives unity to life: The different aspects of personal organisation are an integrated part of spirituality. The spirit by which we do things is different from that of a director of a large firm. We don't organise a pastoral ministry in the same way as we organise a bank. So we are talking about the practical living not only of an organised person but of a spiritual person. Organisation should be integrated into our life-plan.

So a spirituality that gives unity to life can be a powerful motivating force. Activism that leaves no time for cultivating an interior life ends up discharging our batteries. As we face serious problems our interior feelings are ones of emptiness and discouragement. Spirituality gives us interior strength and serenity in face of challenge. Here Jesus is our model. The gospels present him as always resorting to prayer before facing his greatest challenges. And so we strive as if everything depends on us, but know that, in the end, everything depends on God. Motivation cannot depend only on good results. It must go beyond that. No matter how we organise ourselves there will always be failure and deception. But spiritual people do not go into a panic in face of difficulties. They can count on a superior force. They are prepared to plant and leave the harvesting for others. St Paul's spirituality gives our pastoral work with young people a deeper meaning: 'I have planted; Apollo has watered; but it is God who has given the growth.'

Today, psychologists study different personality types. Each personality type has its strong points and its weak points. There are areas of our personality that we can improve and other areas that we have to accept. Some personality types have difficulty with any type of organisation. We all know people who are disorganised in everything they do. Some can improve by studying the suggestions given here; others are not able to do so (I believe these are few). Such people should acknowledge their limitations and not take on functions that demand certain organisational skills. Taking on these functions of co-ordination can lead to frustration and deception because they are unable to meet the expectation of others. The solution is to assume functions that combine with their gifts, rather than taking on responsibilities because of their status-value.

In a successful church ministry, different personality types compliment each other. Different gifts contribute to the well being of the whole body. It is important to evaluate your personality and temperament and adopt an organisational style with which you are comfortable. Some, for example, work well under pressure and with deadlines; other are crippled under pressure. Some can concentrate for long periods; others need frequent breaks.

Appendix No. 21A:

Suggested picture for the Social Shortsightedness Exercise

Painting of the Haitian artist Jacques Chéry showing the universal mission of Christ and the church in face of the challenges of today's world.

Appendix No. 21B:

The Eclipse of the Sun

The Captain to the First Sergeant
Tomorrow there will be an eclipse of the sun, something that doesn't happen everyday. Order the company to stand in formation, at 7 o'clock, in instruction uniform. In this way, everyone can observe the phenomenon of which we will give an explanation. If it rains, it wouldn't be possible to see anything and the men will remain in formation in the lodgings, awaiting the roll call.

The First Sergeant to the Second Sergeant
By order of the captain there will be an eclipse of the sun tomorrow. The captain will give an explanation at 7 o'clock, something that doesn't happen everyday. If it rains there will be no roll call outside. The eclipse will be in the lodgings.

The Second Sergeant to the Corporal
Tomorrow, at 7 o'clock, an eclipse of the sun will come to the barracks in marching uniform. If there is no rain, something that doesn't happen everyday, the captain will give an explanation in the lodgings.

Corporal to the Soldiers
Attention: Tomorrow at 7 o'clock, the captain will do an eclipse of the sun, in civil clothes, and will give an explanation. You will be in formation in the lodgings, something that doesn't happen everyday. If it rains there will be no roll call.

Among the Soldiers
The corporal said that tomorrow the sun will do an eclipse for the captain, in civil clothes, and he will ask it for an explanation. This thing is likely to provoke a good row, one of those things that happens everyday. With God's help, it will rain.

Appendix No.22:

Evaluation of the TCL

1. What did you like most about this course?

2. What did you discover in this course?

3. What did you find most important for your life? Give examples.

4. Is there any part of this course that could have been better? Explain your answer.

Appendix No. 23A:

Celebration of Commitment

Initial observation

Many of our celebrations are often too intellectual and as a result do not motivate, especially a younger generation.

Emotions are important in celebrations, especially for young people. It is important that people have an experience of different types of celebrations: some more joyful and energising, others more meditative. Celebrations should involve the different dimensions of people's lives: intellectual, emotional, imaginative and corporal. We communicate with God and with others with all our being. 'You must love the Lord your God with all your heart, with all your soul, and with all your mind … and your neighbour as yourself' (Mt 22:37-39). In this celebration we will give some suggestions on how to do this.

Often, in retreats and courses, celebrations are prepared by a team of volunteers, based on their own ideas and experiences. This celebration follows a different logic. The plan, theme, gesticulations, symbols and reflections have been prepared beforehand. While people are free to make the changes they judge necessary, in general, we recommend that no major changes be made. This celebration has been used in many courses and has been an important spiritual experience for many people.

There are different motives for preparing the celebration beforehand. The liturgical teams made up of volunteers, during retreats and courses, often lack experience and material. Many lay people don't know how to prepare a celebration. They never had an opportunity to learn. They never learned at home and never learned in the parish or school. Also, during a course, material is generally not readily available, there is little time and it is difficult to give adequate training. On the other hand, lay people and especially youth, learn to celebrate, celebrating – and not just listening to talks on the importance of celebration.

This celebration aims to help people have an experience of a well-prepared and meaningful celebration that has good content and is, at the same time, creative. This experience can serve as a reference point to for other moments, when participants have to prepare celebrations on their own. Obviously, this isn't the only model of celebration possible. We need to prepare other models so that people can have a wider experience.

I believe we should use both options in our courses and retreats: celebrations that are prepared beforehand and others that are prepared by volunteers, during the event. Both approaches complement each other.

1. Entrance
> **Welcomers:**
> A member of the liturgical team welcomes people at the entrance to the place of worship and, at the same time, hands out cards of different colours to be used during the penitential act (participants should have been told beforehand to bring pens). Another member of the team wets her hands in a basin of water perfumed with flowers and touches the face of the participant, as a sign of welcome, while, at the same time, saying some words of welcome.

2. Within: initial atmosphere:
> **Those responsible for the preparation of the ambience and the sound:**
> The *physical ambience* should be prepared beforehand to create an atmosphere of celebration, a sacred space where the Pascal mystery will be enacted, a sense of reaching out to something beyond.
>
> *Background music.* Before the participants enter the place of worship, background music is played to create an atmosphere that favours silence, personal reflection and communication with the Lord.
>
> *Flame.* A flame in the centre creates a special ambience. A flame is an important symbol. Symbols communicate on a more profound level than the word and the discourse. It has the capacity to connect us with God, with the life we celebrate and with the commitment that we take on. The burning flame creates an ambience which is propitious for interior reflection.
>   The flame can be prepared in the following way: Fibreglass is placed in a heat resistant clay vessel and a litre of alcohol is poured over it. The fibreglass is then lighted. Fibreglass has the advantage that it can be used many times over and doesn't make the vessel too warm.
>   While this part of the celebration is more meditative, other parts can be more joyful. It is important to unite festive celebration and interior life.
>
> *Seats* are organised in a circle. A space should be left for those who would like to sit on the ground. If there is no carpet on the floor, pillows, cushions, mattresses or blankets can be used.

3. Greeting
> **Priest:** In the name of the Father ...

4. Remembering Life
> **Priest:**
> The priest makes an introduction to the celebration and asks the group to remember the important events, the people who are absent, the feast of the day, the liturgical time. It is a concrete way of placing prayer into the context of life and of bringing life into prayer. It is not yet the time for the prayers of the faithful. It is especially a moment for putting oneself in tune with the body of the church and with all the people of God who are walking on the road of life as a pilgrim church.

5. *Penitential Rite*

Person responsible for Penitential Rite:
Preparation of the setting:
- Cross laid out on the ground
- Utensil or clay vessel with some matches
- Background music (cassette or CD)

Motivation: this part should not be read mechanically, but rather communicating the meaning of the text.
Sin exists within and outside of us.
Evil entered the world and, like an intruding thief, took over the best of us: the mind and the heart (thoughts and affection). We don't really think as we should ('Your thoughts are not my thoughts, says the Lord'), neither do we love one another as brothers and sisters. Many times, we have given way to lies and used masks and brought about disunion around us. The fruit of sin is death (not life)! We need a *liberator*!

Each one takes up his/her small card and pen.

Look within yourself, at your conscience.
Look at society, at the world and at yourself and write, in a word or a phrase, the sin or an individual situation of sin – to be burned later.

Silence – Background music

Each one reflect on what you have written and that for which you are now sorry and then put it in the vase to be burnt. Sing a hymn that asks for pardon. It is our cry for the mercy of God, to free us from all sin. The Lord welcomes us as the father who opens his arms, his house and his heart to the son who has returned.

Priest:
May almighty god have mercy on us, pardon our sins and bring us to eternal life.

All are invited to shake the hands of the person beside you, in a gesture of reconciliation.

Prayer 'Collect' (1st prayer)

6. *First reading* (to be chosen by the liturgical team)

7. *Gospel Acclamation and Biblical Reading*
Persons responsible for the music, the reader and the overhead projector:
Select a suitable hymn and sing the chorus.

At this moment let us welcome the living Word of God.
- It is important that some gesture be made that brings out the central place of the Bible in our lives. The reader or a group, for example, can enter doing a liturgical dance, dancing or swaying and with the Bible held up, while at the same time, a hymn of acclamation of the gospel is sung.

- The reader reads the biblical text in such a way that it comes across as a living message – a good news. We suggest the text of The Disciples of EmMaus (Luke 24:13-35).
  The projection of the biblical text on the wall, with an overhead projector, facilitates the understanding of the messaging and sharing in the group. A sheet of paper can be placed underneath the transparency and slowly pulled back to reveal the message that is being read. The suspense helps to maintain the attention of the listeners.
- After the reading, the acclamation hymn is sung again and the reader moves around with the Bible held up in a liturgical dance.

8. *Meditation*
   Priest, overhead projector and sound:
   - After the reading, a time of silence is necessary to allow the word to reverberate within us. The participants remain in silence while some background music or hymn is played. Transparencies with different images (if possible in colours) can be projected on the walls with an overhead projector.

9. *Sharing of the Word*
   Priest and overhead projector:
   - The person responsible for the overhead projector projects the gospel text again on the wall to facilitate the sharing.
   - The president of the celebration invites the participants to share their ideas on the message in the reading, by linking the gospel message with the life situations around them. God reveals himself through two books: the Book of the Bible and the Book of Life.

10. *Prayer of the Faithful*
    The priest and the person responsible for the singing:
    The Word of God points to the distance that exists between the reality of life around us and God's plan. In the prayers we ask that the reign of God may come, that the Lord will encourage us in our effort to build a better world. It is the moment to present our brothers and sisters to the Father, to intercede for humanity.
    After each 2 or 3 spontaneous prayers, we can sing a refrain of a hymn that is known by all, in the form of a 'Mantra' (repeating three or four times and always singing in a lower volume and finally singing with closed lips, humming. The 'Mantra' should be practised beforehand with everyone). Please check the instructions for the Saturday morning prayer.

11. *Offertory*
    Persons responsible for the symbols and the singing:
    Objects that symbolise what the course meant to participants are presented in the offertory procession. When the priest raises the host, the refrain of an offertory hymn is sung. The same refrain is repeated when he raises the chalice.
    Suggested hymn:
    Holy, Holy, Holy …

12. Eucharistic Prayer: Consecration
> ***Person responsible for the overhead projector:***
> During the Eucharistic Prayer we can turn off all lights, leaving only the light of the overhead projector turned on. At the moment of consecration the person responsible for the overhead projector can project onto the wall an image linked with the Last Supper or the sacrifice of Calvary.

13. Our Father
> ***The priest and the person responsible for the singing:***
> The Our Father can be sung, using an attractive melody. If necessary the words can be projected on the wall.

14. Communion
> ***The priest and the persons responsible for the sound and the overhead projector:***
> It is recommended that the Communion Service takes place in an environment of silence. Some background music can facilitate an environment of interior reflection and personal prayer.
>
> During the communion the person responsible for the overhead projector can project an image linked to this moment.

15. Ceremony of sending on Mission (after the Communion)
> ***Persons responsible for the ceremony (a couple), for the sound and the singing:***
> Two members of the team (a couple) preside at the ceremony of the unction of the hands as a gesture of sending the participants back to their community on mission. This ceremony is divided into three parts:
>   a. Meditation on the significance of our hand
>   b. Ceremony of unction of the hands
>   c. Blessing of sending on mission
>
> After a short motivation, one of the members does a meditation on the significance of our hands. Some background music is played while he (she) speaks. The following text can be used or modified.

a. Meditation on the hands

> Background music – every one stands in a large circle. If there are too many people for one circle, then two concentric circles can be formed.
>
> ***Facilitator: Meditation on the hands***
> Participants are asked to stand in a circle for the meditation.
> Look at your hands. They are hands that can open to welcome, to caress, to bless, to serve, to shake the hands of others, as a sign of solidarity. These hands make us remember other hands. They are hands that come together to pray: hands of children, of young people, of adults, of old people. They are hands of surgeons that save lives. They are the hardened hands of workers who contribute to building our country, but are not appreciated. They are hands of farm workers who, through their work, provide the food on our tables. They are the hands of young

typists who move with incredible speed. They are the hands of musicians who raise our spirits, of writers who inspire us. They are the hands of technicians who fix our computers, our tape recorders, our televisions and our cars. They are the hands of painters who project us beyond time and space. They are the hands that caress, of mothers, of fiancées, of spouses.

But these hands, capable of so many gestures that raise us, are also capable of gestures that oppress. They are the hands that are raised to attack, to reject, to despise, to strike or take away life. They are the hands that close the door to others. They are lazy hands that refuse to help.

Look closely at the contours of your hands. That these hands may always be at the service of good, as were the hands of Jesus!

Now touch and hold the hands of the persons at your side. Pass energy to the other person with your right hand and receive energy form the others through the left hand. This energy is the divine energy of God who uses us as transmitters.

Now, all raise your hands together – slowly – opening yourself to the power of God who wishes to build a 'new heaven' and a 'new land'. 'Lord, we are your instruments to build a New World. Make us the instruments of your peace. According to your will.'

Still with your hands raised, the person responsible for the singing begins to sing the refrain of a well known hymn.

Suggested Refrain:

b. Ceremony of unction of the hands and the giving of the symbol of commitment
The two facilitators responsible invite the participants to come forward so that their hands may be anointed with oil as a sign of being sent back to their communities in mission. Common oil can be used (e.g. cooking oil, olive oil). The anointing of the hands symbolises the preparation of the hands for work, for commitment, for solidarity. We need to soil our hands.

As a sign of the commitment that each participant is undertaking, the two facilitators give each participant a symbol of commitment (a cross, a badge, etc). [Symbols are important, especially for young people. Symbols have deep roots in human psychology, as they work with the emotions and the imagination. They frequently have more power for bringing about change, for bringing about commitment and dedication, than the purely rational. Every organisation of any importance has a symbol or a brandmark through which it is immediately identified. In our pastoral ministry we need to work more with symbols to have greater effect. The symbols can be place in a decorated basket to emphasise their importance and blessed with Holy Water before being given out to each participant.]

It is important that the symbol chosen be something that can be used afterwards in public. We suggest that a special badge or cross be chosen (See the design of do Appendix 39).

During the ceremony the person responsible for the singing can start a hymn to be taken up by all.
Suggested hymn:

c. *Blessing of sending on mission*
Commentary: Now that our hands have been anointed and we have been sent out on mission, let us ask the Lord for his blessing as we follow in his footsteps.

Let us invoke the blessing of God who is Father and Mother over all who have come together here, so that there be no disunion, drugs, racism, violence, poverty, and injustice, in summary that life no longer be threatened.

Place your right hand on the shoulder of the person at your side and repeat:

May God Father and Mother give you:
The courage of Moses to face oppression – the perseverance of John the Baptist – the enthusiasm of Magdalene;
The vitality of the Prophets, to awaken the hope that is sleeping in the hearts of young people:
The availability of Mary at the moment of her Yes. Her simplicity to listen to the pleas and cry of the people;
The testimony of the first Christians;
The certainty and the faith of the martyrs (names . . .);
The decision and the availability of the poor to answer the call of God;
That young people have a strong heart to love, a strong heart to pardon;
Be joyful in your commitments, in your participation, in the difficulties, persevering in the ministry you have taken on and show solidarity for those who have fallen away. Be joyful with those who are joyful and cry with those who are crying.
Don't allow yourself to be carried away by evil, but rather overcome evil with good.
Finally, Lord, so that we can, both within and outside our pastoral ministry, take on the task of transforming our society into a society where there are equal opportunities for all, a fraternal society where all have both a voice and place – as we walk on the way to your Reign. Amen.

May the Lord bless you;
May the Lord protect you;
May the Lord give you peace.

16. *Prayer*:
The president of the assembly or the priest makes a short prayer summarising the celebration and in the name of all presents this to the Father, through Christ, in the unity of the Holy Spirit.

17. Final blessing of the priest

> May the Lord bless us and keep us! Lord may your light shine over us and be favourable! Lord turn your face to us and give us peace! May the Lord confirm the work of our hands, now and for ever. Amen!

18. Kiss of Peace

Appendix No. 23B:

The Road to Emmaus
Luke 24:13-35

That very same day, two of them were on their way to a village called Emmaus, seven miles from Jerusalem, and they were talking together about all that had happened. Now as they talked this over, Jesus himself came up and walked by their side; but something prevented them from recognising him. He said to them, 'What matters are you discussing as you walk along?' They stopped short, their faces downcast.

Then one of them, called Cleophas, answered him, 'You must be the only person staying in Jerusalem who does not know the things that have been happening there these last few days.' 'What things?' he asked. 'All about Jesus of Nazareth,' they answered 'who proved he was a great prophet by the things he said and did in the sight of God and of the whole people; and how our chief priests and our leaders handed him over to be sentenced to death, and had him crucified. Our own hope had been that he would be the one to set Israel free. And this is not all: two whole days have gone by since it all happened; and some women from our group have astounded us: they went to the tomb in the early morning, and when they did not find the body, they came back to tell us they had seen a vision of angels who declared he was alive. Some of our friends went to the tomb and found everything exactly as the women had reported, but of him they saw nothing.'

Then he said to them, 'You foolish men! So slow to believe the full message of the prophets! Was it not ordained that the Christ should suffer and so enter into his glory?' Then, starting with Moses and going through all the prophets, he explained to them the passages throughout the scriptures that were about himself.

When they drew near to the village to which they were going, he made as if to go on; but they pressed him to stay with them. 'It is nearly evening,' they said, 'and the day is almost over.' So he went in to stay with them. Now while he was with them at table, he took the bread and said the blessing; then he broke it and handed it to them. And their eyes were opened and they recognised him; but he had vanished from their sight. Then they said to each other, 'Did not our hearts burn within us as he talked to us on the road and explained the scriptures to us?'

They set out that instant and returned to Jerusalem. There they found the Eleven assembled together with their companions, who said to them, 'Yes, it is true. The Lord has risen and has appeared to Simon.' Then they told their story of what had happened on the road and how they had recognised him at the breaking of bread.

Appendix No. 23C:

Distribution of functions for the Celebration of Commitment

General Co-ordinator: _____

President of Celebration (celebrant): _____

Preparation of setting: _____

Initial welcome: _____

Penitential Rite: _____

Biblical Reading: _____

Sound: _____

Overhead projector: _____

Singing: _____

Ceremony of sending on mission: _____

Symbols for the offertory procession: _____

Preparation of material
- Tape recorder, CD, cassettes
- Overhead projector
- Material for flame: 2 clay vessels, fibre glass, one litre of alcohol,
- One small bowl with olive oil or some other type of oil
- Small basket with the symbols of commitment
- Transparencies with the gospel reading and with different coloured pictures or images and the final blessing
- Preparation of setting for Mass: necessary material for the Mass, rugs, tapestry, flowers, posters etc.

Appendix No. 24:

Form for Financial Report

Course:_____

Place:_____

Date:_____

FINANCIAL STATEMENT

DATE	DESCRIPTION	IN	OUT	BALANCE

Appendix No. 25:

Model of badge as Symbol of Commitment
(To be given out in the final celebration)

Appendix No. 26:

Model of name-tag

Name:

Number:

Appendix No. 27:

A Pastoral Experience:
Using the TCL as a Tool for Pastoral Renewal

George Boran

During the nineties I worked with the Hispanic Youth Ministry in a diocesan centre in the United States. During that time I was finishing a doctorate in the area of leadership, before returning to Brazil. There were more than 300 thousand Hispanic people in the diocese, the majority young people. Most of these young people were born in different Latin American countries; others were descendants of immigrants from the southern continent.

In conjunction with the diocesan co-ordination team I prepared this evaluation, at the request of the diocese. This course, the TCL (Training Course for Leaders) played an important part in this pastoral experiment.

Obviously pastoral experiences cannot be transplanted, without any adaptations, to another soil. The peculiar conditions of the soil in each place, where the experiment is being implanted, need to be taken into account. Even so, there is much similarity between many of the challenges we face and the pastoral strategies that are effective.

1. Initial difficulties

We started the experiment with a diocesan pastoral team. A diagnosis of the situation revealed difficulties that were impeding the growth of an effective youth ministry.
1. The majority of the participants in the diocesan co-ordination had no concrete work with youth on parish level. The first challenge that we faced, therefore, was to link the co-ordination team to the grassroots.
2. There was lack of continuity between meetings. The ideas and decisions at meetings were not being registered. Decisions taken at meetings were subsequently ignored. The lack of continuity created a problem of credibility in the diocese.
3. There was a difficulty in motivating young people at grassroots level. Few people showed up at the different events that were promoted – 15 to 20 people only. The diocesan youth minister was asking a difficult question: 'Is it worth wasting so much energy for such a meagre result?'
4. The co-ordination team lacked leadership skills: how to organise, co-ordinate a meeting, plan, evaluate and accompany the young people systematically.
5. There was no global pastoral vision, both short and long term, that could give some sort of direction to the different initiatives taken.

The challenge, therefore, was to find the more dynamic leaders, connect the co-ordination team with the grassroots, organise a network of youth communities or groups, train young people in the necessary leadership skills and develop a process where young people could feel they were the protagonists (principal actors) and evangelisers of other youth. It was important that youth should have some sort of ownership, otherwise it would be difficult to motivate them.

2. Initial strategy
Initially we considered the possibility of using two different strategies: visiting the parishes and inviting the leaders to come to the meeting of the co-ordination team. Previous experiences of visiting parishes had given very little result. The effects of visits usually disappeared within weeks. Previous experience also showed that the attempt to invite leaders to diocesan meetings had not worked. Either the leaders failed to accept the invitation because they were not motivated or those who did show up didn't persevere. There was no diocesan vision, there were no emotional bonds between people, and there was no vision of youth ministry that offered to widen the restricted horizons of the local youth group. More difficult still was the challenge of the parishes that had no pastoral work with young people. There was need for a strategy that would motivate a generation of youth strongly influenced by a post-modern culture that emphasised the importance of the concrete, subjective values and immediate results.

We decided on a strategy that later produced excellent results. We needed to start with something concrete that would produce immediate results and be successful. We opted to promote this course (Training Course for Leaders, TCL) in the different parishes. This course has different characteristics that makes it useful as an initial strategy for dealing with the difficulties mentioned above: a small team of four people was sufficient to organise it, the financial cost for the participants was low and the course involved everyone as active participants.

The objectives of the course are:
- To train the monitors themselves in leadership skills. In each course, the co-ordination team involved new monitors. Leadership formation is based on the principle that the best way for a person to learn something or acquire a new skill is to create a situation where s/he is obliged to teach it to others. As the monitors acquire these skills and habits they automatically transferred them to other pastoral situations: meetings of co-ordination teams, planning, evaluation, organising activities.
- The leaders acquire important habits for an effective youth ministry: serious preparation, personal organisational habits, team work, capacity to reflect, to diagnose the causes of difficulties being faced, of finding solutions, of guaranteeing continuity through a process of personal and systematic follow up.
- To train beginners in leadership skills.
- To be a tool for reaching parishes where there is an organised youth ministry but which is not connected to the diocesan organisation and to integrate these groups in a network of youth communities on diocesan level.
- To be a tool for forming youth groups in parishes or communities where there is no youth work. This involves a strategy of inviting young people to the course and, at the end of the course, proposing continuity as a youth group or as part of some other youth organisation.
- To help leaders to bond together on a diocesan and parish level.
- The course is based on four themes: Group Dynamics, The Dignity of the Human Person, Jesus Christ and the Church as Community. The different exercises help the young people to connect the bible to the concrete situations of their daily lives.

3. Consequences and Other Pastoral Strategies

a. A New Organisation

New leadership emerged through the different courses: a leadership that was responsible, enthusiastic and dedicated. The need to rethink the organisational structures of the diocesan youth ministry now became evident. It was decided to form three structures on diocesan level: a Central Committee, a Diocesan Council, and a Formation Team.

The *Central Committee* was made up of eight people who met monthly to reflect on future direction, to prepare the meeting of the Diocesan Council and to co-ordinate the meeting of the Council. Each member of the committee had a function and a specific responsibility: recreational activities, courses, communication ... The Central Committee was seen as the 'think-tank' of the youth ministry.

The *Formation Team* was made up of twelve people. This number continues to grow as new monitors are trained. The members of the Formation Team were not a separate group, but also continued participating in the other levels of youth ministry in order to avoid the danger of forming a parallel movement. This team continually trained new members. Four or five people were selected to give each course, one of them being the general co-ordinator.

The *Diocesan Council* was made up of representatives of the parish groups. Normally two or three representatives from each parish participated in the monthly meeting where all important decisions were taken.

We followed an important pedagogical principle of youth work. If you wish to motivate and form youth who are responsible you have to give them responsibility. This is a principle that appears in many of the church documents: the young person should be the first evangeliser of other young people.

b. Communication

From the beginning we gave special priority to communications. We believed that the efficacy of our pastoral work would depend largely on our capacity to facilitate the channels of communication between youth ministry and the rest of the church. We made lists of names, addressees and telephones of the members of the Central Committee, of the Diocesan Council, of the Formation Team and of the participants in courses, and gave copies to all. The members of the Diocesan Council received, beforehand, by mail, the invitation and agenda of the monthly meeting. Members, also, began participating in television and radio programmes run by the diocesan communication office and writing for the diocesan newspaper. We started a simple news bulletin as a tool for communicating between the youth groups.

c. Annual Calendar

We elaborated an annual calendar and planning process to integrate the different diocesan activities so as not to overburden the same people. There was a danger of becoming involved in many meetings without a long-term vision and concrete strategies for implementing this vision.

d. Results

After a year and a half the results were impressive. The members of the Central Committee had taken on responsibility for running the youth ministry with dedication. There was a division of responsibilities and each member carried out his/her function

ORGANISATIONAL CHART

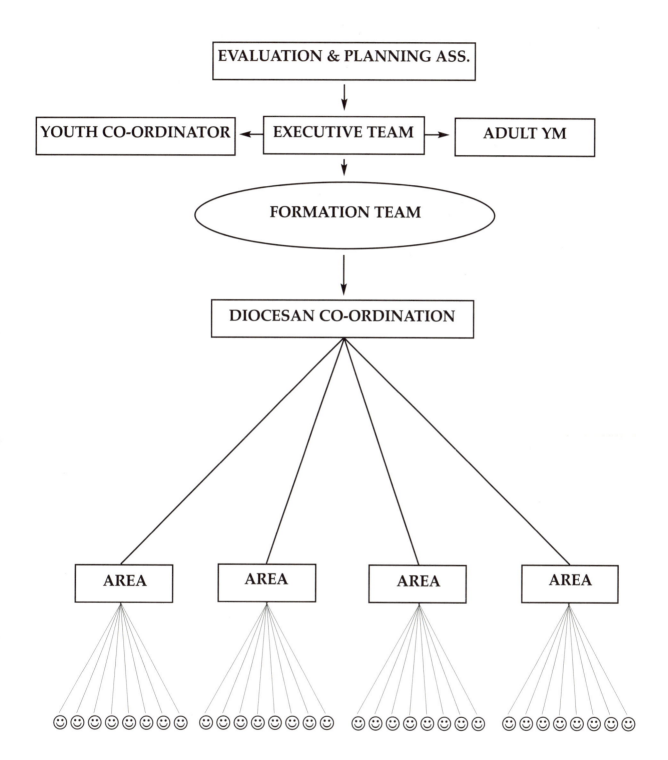

with enthusiasm and efficiency. The Diocesan Council was continually integrating new parishes. New leaders emerged. Motivation grew due to the process of involvement in decision making.

The first activity that the Council organised was a get together to celebrate their common Hispanic cultural roots. The co-ordination team did a very effective advertising job. More than 200 youth showed up. A dance for the New Year was a success. Both events had the aim of strengthening the bonds of friendship between the youth groups in the diocese and solidify their identity as members of a common diocesan ministry. A second level course was also a success.

e. Dangers to be avoided
i) *A few people being overburdened*. To the extend that the diocesan youth ministry grows there is the danger that the principal leaders take on too many commitments and end up suffering from burn out and then drop out altogether. Generosity and enthusiasm push them to want to take on everything at the same time. The solution depends on two factors: delegation and planning. There is need for continually forming and involving new leaders so that responsibilities are better distributed. An annual plan/calendar makes it possible to distribute activities and programmes and avoid concentrating events around the same period of time.
ii) *Tension between Co-ordination Team and Grassroots*. At times, it is easier to work on diocesan level. The workshops, the courses, the youth encounters, the retreats, the meetings and the contact with youth from different places can generate a lot of enthusiasm. Those on co-ordination level can easily forget the work on grass roots level: the group meetings, the formation of new groups, the personal accompaniment of members, the preparation of meetings, formation material and the organisation of some sort of action on local level. The best leaders may dedicate all their time to the diocesan work and abandon direct contact with the grassroots' groups, while, at the same time, forgetting to prepare others to take their place. And so the groups enter a period of crisis. There is, therefore, a constant tension between the work on diocesan level and the work on grassroots' level. A balance is necessary to strengthen both. If we weaken the groups on grassroots level, we end up with a lot of generals without any troops. When we need to mobilise the troops only the generals appear. If on the other hand, we only work on grassroots level, we lack a wider vision and we fail to accumulate experience and learn from others. Isolation usually leads to greater poverty in terms of growth. We stagnate rather than going forward.

6. What is lacking and what are our goals?
At this stage of the experiment the following recommendations were presented to the Diocesan Council:
a) We need to reach more parishes in the diocese and connect them to the diocesan ministry. For this reason we are working on a project called 'twinning parishes': the parishes that participate are given the task of contacting another parish and involving them in the diocesan ministry.
b) The present structures (Central Committee, Diocesan Council, Formation Team) have a limited capacity for involving young people on grass roots level in decision making. There is a danger that a small group will become the 'owner' of the diocesan youth ministry if there are not some other structures to involve a greater number of people in the decision making process. An important structure is still missing: an evaluation and planning assembly. There is need, therefore, to organise a biannual assembly. An assembly

has two characteristics that distinguish it from other encounters or courses: the participants are delegates elected by other youth in the parishes and an assembly has a decision-making character. The Diocesan Council itself would be subordinated to the decisions of the assembly. But, in order to prepare and co-ordinate an assembly of this type, there is need for a specialised facilitator: someone who understands the methodology of planning and is able to co-ordinate an assembly of this type where the confrontation between different experiences and ideas can lead to concrete proposals for the future direction of youth ministry.

c) With time we need to organise a diocesan retreat to help us develop a deeper spirituality in youth ministry.

d) The youth groups and co-ordination teams need to include a Review of Life as part of their annual calendar – at least one per year. A Review of Life can take different forms, but basically it provides an opportunity for young people to talk about their personal lives, in the light of the gospel. Frequently, in meeting of co-ordination commissions, the emphasis is on organising different events and there is no opportunity for the young people to talk interior dramas they are facing as adolescents. When not dealt with, these interior dramas and personal problems often come to the surface and explode, forcing the young person to abandon everything.

e) There is a need to begin a process of elaborating principles and guidelines for Hispanic youth ministry in order to avoid dispersion of energies and so that people are clear about where they are going (goals), and how to get there (methodology or strategy).

f) We need to work more on the formation of a critical sense and the option for the poor as demanded by the social doctrine of the church.

g) The youth ministry receives funds from the diocese to organise youth ministry. As the youth ministry grows this money will no longer be sufficient. It is necessary also to work toward financial independence. There are different motives for this option. When a ministry is partially financed by its members there is a greater sense of ownership and responsibility. Financial independence offers a solution to the difficulties created by the insufficient funds available from the diocese and to the danger of these funds being cut off entirely from one moment to another. On the other hand, diocesan help is also important as a visible sign of commitment of the local church to the work with young people.

h) As more and more parishes become part of the diocesan youth ministry it will be necessary to also organise smaller units (or deaneries).

i) An important task for youth ministry, on grass roots' level, is the organisation of some sort of action. Action can be either in the community or outside of it. A special concern should be Hispanic youth who are marginalised, who don't have work or a place to live, and who need legal help as non documented immigrants.

Conclusion
There is much to be done. The danger is to think that everything has to be done at once. The desire to embrace everything at the same time inevitably leads to superficiality. Therefore, the goals outlined above should be part of a plan over several years. A house is not built in a day; neither is it built by starting with the roof. It is built by starting with the foundation and then placing one brick at a time, until the whole building is completed. An effective youth ministry follows the same principles.